What people are saying about

Nature's Sacrament

David McDuffie has written an engaging book the rich relationship between a   e epic of evolution. He opens up   ction that has implications for h   Earth community. We are all in his   ...ul contribution to ecotheology.

Mary Evelyn Tucker, Yale University, coauthor of *Ecology and Religion* and *Journey of the Universe*

By showing us how the Eucharist and the Incarnation lead us to an awareness of God's presence in all things and how an appreciation of the evolutionary history of the world deepens our understanding of the Eucharist, David McDuffie shows how a common experience of wonder, awe and appreciation in the natural world can bring together those scientists who do not profess religious faith and those Christians who may not have appreciated evolutionary processes. As such McDuffie has provided a needed service to both groups at a critical time in history.

Robin Gottfried, Director, Center for Religion and Environment at Sewanee: The University of the South

David McDuffie has focused on what must be the heart of Christian ecotheology – the nexus between Jesus and the sacramental reality of the Earth. For way too long Christians have been unwilling to embrace this nexus with passion and intelligence to the detriment of our collective faith and the health of the planet. This book makes an important, timely, thoughtful contribution to the growing conversation in this area.

Fletcher Harper, Executive Director, GreenFaith

Nature's Sacrament

The Epic of Evolution and a Theology
of Sacramental Ecology

Nature's Sacrament

The Epic of Evolution and a Theology of Sacramental Ecology

David C. McDuffie

CHRISTIAN ALTERNATIVE
BOOKS

Winchester, UK
Washington, USA

JOHN HUNT PUBLISHING

First published by Christian Alternative Books, 2021
Christian Alternative Books is an imprint of John Hunt Publishing Ltd.,
No. 3 East St., Alresford, Hampshire SO24 9EE, UK
office@jhpbooks.com
www.johnhuntpublishing.com
www.christian-alternative.com

For distributor details and how to order please visit the 'Ordering' section on our website.

ISBN: 978 1 78904 717 2
978 1 78904 718 9 (ebook)
Library of Congress Control Number: 2020948079

A CIP catalogue record for this book is available from the British Library.

Design: Stuart Davies

UK: Printed and bound by CPI Group (UK) Ltd, Croydon, CR0 4YY
Printed in North America by CPI GPS partners

We operate a distinctive and ethical publishing philosophy in all areas of our business, from our global network of authors to production and worldwide distribution.

Contents

To Dr. William L. Power—Professor, Mentor, and Friend

Acknowledgements

I would like to thank the Religious Studies Department at the University of North Carolina at Chapel Hill where the thought process that led to this book began and early work on it was done. I would also like to thank The School of Theology at Sewanee: The University of the South where these early ideas were expanded and developed further toward what became the present volume.

I am grateful to the following individuals who read and provided valuable suggestions and insight on either individual chapters or the entire text as it was being written: Norman Wirzba at Duke University; Don Saliers at Emory University; Bruce Morrill at Vanderbilt University; and Cynthia Crysdale, Benjamin King, Robert MacSwain, and Andrew Thompson at Sewanee: The University of the South. To Robin Gottfried at Sewanee, Ann Somers at the University of North Carolina at Greensboro, Mary Evelyn Tucker at Yale University, and Joyce Wilding, thank you for helpful and encouraging conversations along the way. To the late Frank Golley at the University Georgia, who introduced me to the academic study of Ecology, thank you for introducing me to a broader appreciation of the connectedness of life and awakening me to the possibilities available when one recognizes that religion and evolutionary biology can be quite compatible.

To my students, particularly at the University of North Carolina at Chapel Hill and the University of North Carolina at Greensboro, I have very much enjoyed our conversations on some of the topics covered in the book, and I greatly appreciate you helping me to develop these ideas in the classroom.

I am thankful for my family: my wife Jennie and our three children Aidan, Callum, and Isla. Their patience and love made the completion of this work possible. I am thankful for my parents, Charles and Pat McDuffie, both of whom introduced me to natural theology at an early age each in their own particular way. I also want to thank my brother, Matt, who took me on my earliest trips into the woods. His knowledge of the natural world still far exceeds my own, but I have greatly benefited from following him down the trail.

There are countless others who have contributed something to make this book a possibility. To all who contributed in ways recognized or not, I am truly appreciative.

Finally, I want to express my deep gratitude to Dr. William L. Power, Professor Emeritus of Religion at the University of Georgia, to whom this book is dedicated. He taught me that all truth claims, religious or scientific, should be judged by the critical criteria of reason and experience and that there is no contradiction in valuing and respecting Christian tradition while holding it accountable to maintaining applicability in our contemporary context. While his name does not appear frequently in the following pages, his influence is present throughout. Without this influence, this book would not have been possible.

There is grandeur in this view of life, with its several powers, having been originally breathed into a few forms or into one; and that whilst this planet has gone cycling on according to the fixed law of gravity, from so simple a beginning endless forms most beautiful and most wonderful have been, and are being, evolved.[1]

Introduction

These are the last lines from the 1859 first edition of Charles Darwin's *On the Origin of Species* in which he developed his theory of evolution through natural selection. The culmination of Darwin's work on speciation served to illuminate the realization that all living things (humans included) are connected in one giant web or tree of life that spans millions of years of natural history on Earth. Ironically, Darwin had no understanding of the primary biological factor perpetuating this process. The emergence of the science of genetics unlocked this mystery, and in the more than 150-year interval since the publication of *Origin*, we have been provided with evidence that supports Darwin's brilliant insight. We now know that we are genetically related and ecologically connected to all living things from chimpanzees and bonobos, our closest living relatives with whom we share approximately 99% of our genetic information, to microscopic bacteria. In brief, all living things on our planet are related through our genetic codes, and it is probable that this genetic kinship can be traced back to the emergence of life's common ancestor, the first single celled life on Earth. These developments in the biological sciences combined with the sciences of geology and cosmological physics have revealed to us that we live in an approximately 14-billion-year-old universe on a planet that is approximately 4.6 billion years old and that we are a part of the ongoing process of life that has existed on

Earth for roughly 4 billion years. This is the story of the natural history from which we emerged and of which we are inextricably a part, and it is a narrative that is added to on nearly a daily basis by ongoing scientific investigation.

E. O. Wilson has referred to this narrative as the evolutionary epic and claims that "the evolutionary epic is probably the best myth we will ever have. It can be adjusted until it comes as close to truth as the human mind is constructed to judge the truth."[2] Elsewhere, he claims that "to the degree that we come to understand other organisms, we will place a greater value on them, and on ourselves."[3] The implication here is that an awareness of ecological connectedness will lead to a greater valuation and concern for the diversity of life on Earth of which we are only a part. This narrative has been adopted by others such as Thomas Berry and Ursula Goodenough who claim that the Epic of Evolution has not only scientific but also religious significance in terms of how it achieves the attribution of ecological value. For instance, Berry describes the scientific narrative of the story of the universe as a manifestation of Divine revelation in order to argue that this "new story of the universe is now needed as our sacred story."[4]

I agree that there is a connection between an understanding of, a valuation for, and, consequently, the protection of the ecological connections that sustain all forms of life, and the purpose of the following book will be to examine the ways in which the emerging narrative of the universe's natural history can be correlated with and enhance the sacramental tradition of the Christian church.[5] More specifically, I will focus on the religious and ecological significance of the "Epic of Evolution" in an effort to seamlessly connect the ecological value attributed as a part of this scientific narrative with the grace understood to be present in Christian sacramental worship with a particular emphasis on the Eucharist. I will argue that the sacramental emphasis on grace being conveyed through material reality, in conversation with the acceptance of ecological value as demonstrated in the Epic of Evolution, provides the potential for Christian sacramental tradition to make a significant contribution to conserving the threatened ecological communities of our planet.

In a conversation I had a number of years ago with the Rev. Dr. Jerry Cappel, current Director of Province IV Environmental Ministries of the Episcopal Church, he said that it was time that "we move ecology from the committee to the pew" in order for it to be seen as a primary aspect of Christian formation and not just another peripheral issue of concern for the church. The following pages are my attempt to do just that. The potential religious implications of the Epic of Evolution have been well documented, but I will provide a more thorough examination of how the value associated with the evolutionary epic relates specifically to an understanding of Christian sacramental grace. The justification for valuation will emerge from the very heart of the tradition itself and will therefore provide a response to contemporary ecological concerns that is both uniquely Christian and applicable to the global environmental efforts to adequately address these concerns. The overall goal will be to provide a framework for clergy and laity that will assist in envisioning the protection and conservation of the ecological communities of our planet not as a peripheral or additional theological concern but as an integral part of the sacramental life of the church. In essence, nature is the sacrament that undergirds all the sacraments. You cannot have baptism without clean water or Eucharist without the grace that produces healthful wine and bread. The priest is not creating a grace by speaking the words of the sacramental liturgy but is instead revealing a grace that is already present. If all things come from God, then the Earth and life on Earth has to be of sacramental value.

Chapter One

Nature's Grace: The Epic of Evolution, Religious Naturalism, and the Conservation of Nature[6]

I. Introduction

In his *A Primer for Environmental Literacy*, Dr. Frank Golley, a former Ecology professor of mine at the University of Georgia writes the following: "Philosophers say that we can't move from the *is* to the *ought*. I don't agree. For me it all begins with experience, the first step into the forest, and everything else flows from that."[7] In other words, regarding the attribution of ecological value, the naturalistic fallacy critique does not apply. I agree with Dr. Golley on this point, and in this opening chapter, I will assess the religious significance of this ecological value emerging from an awareness of the connectedness and ecological and genetic kinship of all life on Earth.

Therefore, the purpose of the chapter will be to identify and assess the religious and ecological significance of the acceptance of the Epic of Evolution. In what follows, I will identify examples where naturalism is appealed to as the primary explanation of the origin of Earthly life and primary means of orientation for understanding the human sense of connectedness with others, human and non-human, biotic and abiotic. In brief, I will argue that this naturalistic account of the history of life on our planet has emerged as a new, and for some explicitly religious, cultural narrative of origin and connectedness, and I will demonstrate that what is emerging from awareness and understanding of the scientific story of life on earth is a unique valuation for ecological connectedness, an appreciation of where we came from and a willingness to protect the connections that bind us to all other forms of life. This discussion will provide the foundation for the argument made in subsequent chapters that there is a clear correlation between the value attributed in the Epic of Evolution and the Christian concept of sacramental grace conveyed in Eucharistic worship, a correlation that can enhance scientific and religious approaches to the protection of life on Earth.

II. Narratives of Religion and Science and the Valuation of Nature

Biologist Edward O. Wilson is frequently given credit for coining the term "Epic of Evolution." In his Pulitzer Prize winning *On Human Nature* first published in 1978, he writes that "the evolutionary epic is probably the best myth we will ever have. It can be adjusted until it comes as close to truth as the human mind is constructed to judge the truth."[8] Wilson's understanding of the orienting powers of the "Epic of Evolution" represents an alternative to traditional religious narratives of origin. For Wilson, an effective orienting narrative emerges not from a proper understanding of sacred text or theological tradition but from a proper understanding of nature. In a more recent example, he elaborates as follows: "The true evolutionary epic, retold as poetry, is as intrinsically ennobling as any religious epic. Material reality discovered by science already possesses more content and grandeur than all religious cosmologies combined."[9]

In this sense, the scientific narrative of life seems to clearly replace traditional religious narratives, yet the break is not clean in that Wilson also recognizes the significance of the cultural function of religious narratives in terms of the importance of an orienting story in human culture. While he adamantly rejects the metaphysics of supernatural forms of religious expression, he does not reject the effective function of religious narratives. He writes, "People need a sacred narrative. They must have a sense of larger purpose, in one form or other, however

7

intellectualized."[10] As a result, the awe, beauty, and wonder traditionally associated with religious devotion is maintained but is inspired not by the concept of supernatural presence(s) but instead by a naturalistic account of the Earth's ecology.[11] In describing his adolescent journey from supernatural theism to a complete devotion to natural history, Wilson aptly makes a connection between scientific and religious narratives: "I had no desire to purge religious feelings. They were bred in me; they suffused the wellsprings of my creative life."[12] His primary concern, therefore, is not to eradicate the function of religious narratives but to substitute a new, scientific narrative that will help humans address current trends leading to human induced reduction of biological diversity.[13]

Wilson's greatest concern is promoting a conservation ethic that will protect this global biodiversity. According to him, we have now entered the world's sixth great extinction event, the fifth being the event that led to the extinction of the dinosaurs 65 million years ago, where, if conditions remain the same, half the Earth's known species could either be extinct or seriously threatened by the mid-twenty-first century.[14] With this in mind, Wilson claims that the scientific narrative of evolutionary history is the story that can most effectively achieve the protection of the Earth's biodiversity from the factors that currently threaten it. In his words, "[t]o know this world is to gain proprietary attachment to it. To know it well is to love and take responsibility for it."[15]

Wilson makes no attempt to associate his work with what may be called religious, and I have no intention of making such a claim for him. However, through his use of the religious rhetoric of Nature as sacred and being "vital to our physical and spiritual well-being" as well as through his understanding of the 14–15-billion-year natural history of our universe as a new orienting narrative of origin, he links religious language with the attribution of value to the Earth's diverse life forms and the habitats from which they emerge.[16] Therefore, Wilson's rhetoric is applicable to understanding an emerging aspect of the function of religious language in contemporary culture. Whether it is characterized as "religious" or not, his scientific narrative is clearly worthy of attention for the study of religion and ecology in the sense that the story emerging from the natural sciences has become a candidate for serving the function of traditional religious frameworks and also provides the potential to inspire a reverence and value for the biological diversity of life on Earth through the awareness of the kinship between all forms of life, human and non-human.

Interestingly, many of those who have adopted Wilson's understanding of the Epic of Evolution, which is also frequently referred to as the Universe Story or the Journey of the Universe, have accepted this orienting narrative as an emerging form of religious expression. Like Wilson, these individuals base their narrative on the best available scientific evidence for understanding the history of our universe and the life that has emerged and evolved on Earth; however, unlike Wilson, these authors have been more willing to explicitly speak of it as an expression of religious naturalism.

Prominent examples of the "Epic of Evolution" being used as an explicitly religious narrative include the works of Thomas Berry, Brian Swimme, and Ursula Goodenough. In *The Universe Story*, Berry and Swimme call for a new, science based narrative that will "enable the human community to become present to the larger Earth community in a mutually enhancing manner." Such religious expressions, they claim, "will sensitize people to the story that every river and every star and every animal is telling. The goal is not to read a book; the goal is to read the story taking place all around us."[17] For Berry and Swimme, the primary religious revelation for our time should be one drawn from an understanding of the natural history of our planet, one that is not a canonized set of sacred human writings, but is instead a narrative that is ongoing and growing with increasing scientific knowledge. This will, in turn, provide religious expression with an orientation informed by science and scientific inquiry with a perspective that will go beyond the collection of empirical evidence to an attribution of value for biological connections revealed through scientific discovery.

Similarly, in *The Sacred Depths of Nature*, Goodenough attempts "to present an accessible account of our scientific understanding of Nature and then suggest ways that this account can call forth appealing and abiding religious responses—an approach that can be called religious naturalism."[18] Traditional religious concepts are interpreted through a naturalistic perspective and the understanding of religion is reinterpreted, yet not discarded, in light of the modern scientific evidence of the origins of humanity and the biological kinship that we share with all living things. She justifies her application of religion to a scientific perspective with the following statement:

> And so, I profess my Faith. For me, the existence of all this complexity and awareness and intent and beauty, and my ability to apprehend it, serves as the ultimate meaning and the ultimate value. The continuation of life reaches around, grabs its own tail, and forms a sacred circle that requires no further justification, no Creator, no superordinate meaning of meaning, no purpose other than that the continuation continue until the sun collapses or the final meteor collides. I confess a credo of continuation.[19]

It should be noted that, even though Goodenough does not appeal to any form of theism, her form of religious naturalism does not attempt to prove or disprove the existence of God. Instead, the goal of her perspective is the recognition of value in that which we experience in Nature.[20]

For Goodenough, as for Wilson, Berry, and Swimme, a

greater knowledge of nature leads to a greater valuation of the natural world that sustains life on Earth. She writes, "If we can revere how things are, and can find a way to express gratitude for our existence, then we should be able to figure out, with a great deal of work and good will, how to share the Earth with one another and with other creatures, how to restore and preserve its elegance and grace, and how to commit ourselves to love and joy and laughter and hope."[21] According to Goodenough, what is revealed through our understanding of expanding scientific knowledge is "that we are connected to all creatures. Not just in food chains or ecological equilibria. We share a common ancestor. We share gene receptors and cell cycles and signal-transduction cascades. We share evolutionary constraints and possibilities. We are connected all the way down."[22] Therefore, the understanding of the evolutionary epic as a religious narrative has significant implications as an option for effectively addressing contemporary cases of ecological concern. What I have attempted to do here is to show how this trend is emerging further in a contemporary context and how intimately it connects ecological and religious thought.

III. The Epic of Evolution, Religion, and the Re-enchantment of Nature

The question that must be asked is what, then, is the relationship between this new science based narrative and traditional religious narratives of origin and connectedness that are still very influential in our contemporary context? The answer, I believe, is that it is one of continuity and discontinuity, one of enhancement and not replacement, one of cooperation and not necessarily conflict. For instance, Wilson's 2006 book carrying the rhetorically savvy title *The Creation: An Appeal to Save Life on Earth*, is written as an appeal, through letter form, to a hypothetical Southern Baptist minister to join with the forces of science to protect the Earth's threatened biodiversity. While making a clear distinction between scientific and religious arguments for protecting the Creation, what Wilson refers to as Living Nature, he makes this appeal because, he claims, "religion and science are the two most powerful forces in the world today, including especially the United States. If religion and science could be united on the common ground of biological conservation, the problem would soon be solved."[23] In *Journey of the Universe*, Mary Evelyn Tucker and Brian Swimme express a similar sentiment while maintaining more of a continuity with traditional religious narratives. They write that they intend "not to override or ignore these other stories, but rather to bring into focus the challenge of creating a shared future. The great opportunity before us today is to tell this new universe story in a way that will serve to orient humans with respect to our pressing questions: Where did we come from? Why are we here? How should we live together? How can the Earth community flourish?"[24]

Goodenough and Berry also clearly express this emphasis on making the "Epic of Evolution" a foundational aspect of existing religious narratives of origin. Goodenough writes: "Once we have our feelings about Nature in place, then I believe that we can also find important ways to call ourselves Jews... Christians... Buddhists. Or some of each. The words in the traditional texts may sound different to us than they did to their authors, but they continue to resonate with our religious selves. We know what they are intended to mean."[25] According to Berry in *The Sacred Universe*, the "great spiritual mission of the present is to renew all the traditional religious-spiritual traditions in the context of the integral functioning of the biosystems of the planet."[26] In brief, the thesis is not that science will supersede all forms of religion in an emerging secular age; instead, the scientific narrative of the history of our universe and life on Earth contributes to a new orienting story from which emerges a valuation that will most effectively protect the ecological communities and biodiversity to which we are all inextricably related.

A somewhat controversial aspect of this new narrative is that its adherents are unapologetic in claiming that it has a universal appeal to all human cultures, claims that have been adamantly criticized in the social sciences and humanities. Goodenough explains the universal appeal of such a science based ethic in the following manner: "The Big Bang, the formation of stars and planets, the origin and evolution of life on this planet, the advent of human consciousness and the resultant evolution of cultures—this is the story, the one story, that has the potential to unite us, because it happens to be true."[27] Wilson echoes this understanding in his Foreword to Loyal Rue's *Everybody's Story: Wising Up to the Epic of Evolution*: "Is there a way to evolve a great epic that is at once universal, spiritually satisfying, and above all, truthful? The quest for such an epic is the subject of *Everybody's Story*. Loyal Rue's argument is as bold as it is brief: The way to achieve an epic that unites humanity spiritually, instead of cleaving it, is to compose it from the best empirical knowledge that science and history can provide of the real human story. Spirituality is beneficent to the extent that it is based on verifiable truth. I find his argument persuasive."[28] I say that this particular understanding of universality is only somewhat controversial due to the fact that twentieth- and twenty-first-century scientific evidence has made the evidence for the evolutionary theory of the emergence of Earthly life incontrovertible. The skepticism concerning universality is certainly well founded as a means to avoid cultural hegemony. However, the evidence that we are bound together in a natural history spanning 14–15 billion years is now overwhelming, and for individuals like Wilson and Goodenough, this global kinship among all living things, human and non-human, is undeniable and worth exploring if it results in a greater valuation and consequently care for the living nature upon which we all depend for survival.

The Epic of Evolution, properly understood, can potentially contribute to a recognition of value in what are often volatile natural environments and to an appreciation of our necessarily ecological, interconnected, context. In short, acceptance of the science based narrative of origin and connectedness will help human cultures better address global issues such as pollution, overpopulation and overconsumption, habitat destruction, desertification of portions of the world's oceans, global climate change, deforestation, depletion of biodiversity, which are all interrelated issues and environmental crises affecting us all.

However, many are skeptical that an account based on the modern scientific narrative can effectively serve the cultural function of religious narratives in terms of providing for human longings for, for example, comfort, reverence, meaning and significance. Max Weber referred to the legacy of the rise of modern science following the Protestant Reformation and culminating in the Enlightenment as the "disenchantment of the world."[29] In brief, Weber implied that mystery was removed from the natural world when notions of teleological, divine purpose were replaced by empirical explanations for natural processes. Many theologians and critical theorists have echoed this sentiment. What I have attempted to demonstrate here is that this is not the complete story. With the emergence of the Darwinian story of earthly life, the potential was there for scientific evidence to once again reenchant the world through the connectedness inherent in the very naturalistic explanations that were perceived to be the sources of disenchantment.

Environmental historian Donald Worster correctly points out that, while accepting the suffering, pain, and seemingly gratuitous death and profligate waste in nature, Darwin was able to develop and maintain "an all-embracing reverence for life" through his understanding of the evolutionary story.[30] In other words, the Darwinian understanding of ecological connection, while more sobering and less comforting than classical theistic and Romantic notions of the human-nature relationship, was a source for value and awareness of the orienting kinship of all of life:

> One of the chief lessons, for him [Darwin], was that man had not been created with special care in the image of God; therefore, he is one with all other species in a universal brotherhood of living and dying, which he denies only at the risk of cutting himself off from his psychic and biological roots. It was by no means a perfectly happy relationship,... But in Darwin's view, a shared experience of suffering as well as joy could establish a bond between humanity and all other forms of life.[31]

While one must not overlook the oppressive prejudices of racism, sexism, and cultural hegemony characteristic of forms of Social Darwinism nor the destructive forces of modern science unleashed in the forms of atomic and biological warfare and widespread ecological degradation, these are not necessary interpretations or manifestations of the evolutionary story of life on Earth. Furthermore, we can also move beyond Tennyson's characterization of nature as exclusively "red in tooth and claw."[32] According to those whom I have cited here, an alternative is the cultivation of an awareness of and respect for the vast history of the origins of the universe and life on our planet and the ecological, geographical, and genetic kinship of all that has or ever has had life on our planetary home.

Therefore, the era of disenchantment leads to reenchantment in a contemporary, ecological context. Value flows from this awareness of connection and the wonder that we are and that we can experience life, love, and beauty and strive for the true, the good, and the beautiful in order, in the words of Alfred North Whitehead, "to live, to live well, to live better."[33] Consequently, reenchantment of the world is introduced through that which supposedly disenchanted us from our natural environments. Wilson writes:

> The revolution in astronomy begun by Nicolaus Copernicus in 1543 proved that Earth is not the center of the universe, nor even the center of the solar system. The revolution begun by Darwin was even more humbling: it showed that humanity is not the center of creation, and not its purpose either. But in freeing our minds from our imagined demigod bondage, even at the price of humility, Darwin turned our attention to the astounding power of the natural creative process and the magnificence of its products.[34]

Recognition of this new narrative will result in a new understanding for the study of religion and for anyone, regardless of disciplinary affiliation, who wishes to engage it. The enlightenment disciplinary divisions between religion and science, science and the humanities will still be useful. However, the emergence of nature as primary source for orientation, connection and value will create a new avenue where the boundaries between the disciplines blur and merge into each other, where naturalism is the primary source of religious conceptions of knowledge (whether they are called religious or not), knowledge that is informed by, inseparably related to, predicated upon, and not in contradiction with the best available scientific evidence.

IV. The Question of Connection between the Evolutionary Epic and Religious Tradition

If it is to be realized, I believe that established religious traditions have a significant role to play in cultivating this sense of natural value. Yet, there is still significant work to be done. Some proponents of the Epic of Evolution as an orientation narrative on behalf of the protection of biodiversity have serious doubts concerning the applicability of some of the world's historical religious traditions in relation to the evolutionary and ecological narrative of life on Earth. For example, in *Dark Green Religion: Nature Spirituality and the Planetary Future*, Bron Taylor states "that it would be much easier to develop sustainable societies if religions were firmly grounded in an evolutionary-ecological worldview."[35] However, he is clearly skeptical of traditional religions' ability to do so: "Religious thinkers since Darwin have gone through excruciating contortions in their efforts to graft such a worldview onto their faith traditions,... The result simply fails the laugh test for many if not most scientifically literate people."[36]

In arguing for the merits of the Epic of Evolution or "everybody's story" as an orienting narrative to address modern environmental crises, Loyal Rue accepts that, as "living traditions," Axial age religions "may still find the resources and the will to change in fundamental ways as they absorb the perspective of modern science and feel the impact of the global problematique."[37] However, like Taylor, Rue has serious doubts that these historical traditions can effectively make such a transition while remaining true to their own traditional identities:

> On the one hand, if the Axial traditions fail to assimilate the evolutionary cosmology and the ecocentric morality of everybody's story, then the dual crisis of plausibility and relevance will deepen within these traditions to accelerate their decline. On the other hand, if the Axial traditions succeed in absorbing everybody's story they risk compromising their distinctiveness to the point of appearing superfluous.[38]

Such criticisms imply a heavy burden of proof if established religious traditions are going to remain applicable when placed in conversation with the emerging narrative of life on Earth that unites us all through our common evolutionary history.

It is also true that there is either a reluctance to accept or lack of recognition for the religious significance of the evolutionary epic among those practicing these living traditions. I frequently show students in my Religious Studies classes the film *Journey of the Universe*, which is written by Brian Thomas Swimme and Mary Evelyn Tucker and dedicated in gratitude to Thomas Berry. Toward the beginning of the film, which expertly traces the 14-billion-year history of the universe in less than 60 minutes, Swimme, who serves as narrator, states that "perhaps a new story is emerging in our time, one grounded in contemporary science and yet nourished by the ancient religious wisdom of our planet."[39] While there are subtle connections throughout to many world religious traditions, there are no other explicit references to religion in the remainder of the film aside from a scene in which Swimme enters a small church on the Greek island of Samos to discuss the human fascination with stars. After one of the first times that I showed the film to a class, I asked my students if they identified anything that they would call religious. One of my students raised his hand and said, "There was that one part where he went into that church." The implication was clear from his answer that religion was an activity clearly set apart from the natural world within the built environment of church walls. To further this point, in a conversation I had with a Christian theologian a number of years ago, I was describing the epic of evolution in relation to Goodenough's understanding of this narrative contributing to an emerging religious naturalism. At one point in the conversation, he stated rather bluntly, "I'm not sure that you can call that religion."

In addressing these issues, I would like to refer to an often overlooked aspect of Lynn White, Jr.'s influential 1967 article, "The Historical Roots of our Ecologic Crisis," in which he famously claimed that a Western Christian interpretation of dominion combined with modern science and technology was to blame for our modern ecological problems.[40] White states that human ecology "is deeply conditioned by beliefs about our nature and destiny—that is, by religion."[41] Furthermore, in assessing how we might address current ecological problems, he adds: "Since the roots of our trouble are so largely religious, the remedy must also be essentially religious, whether we call it that or not."[42] The point of including a reference to White's article here is not to examine the merits or weaknesses of his thesis. This has been extensively done in scholarly literature since the publication of his article in the journal *Science* served as a watershed moment for the field of Religion and Ecology. Instead, I want to appeal to White's assumption that a reenvisioned Christianity can potentially be a part of the solution to and not a symptom of the problems we face in protecting the life present in Earth's ecosystems.[43]

In an interview with Robert Wright, the late biochemist and Anglican priest and theologian Arthur Peacocke speaks of his writing opening Christianity up to "the vistas of science and what science is telling us about the natural world." During the interview, he reflects on a visit with his grandchildren to the Rose Center for Earth and Space in New York and walking through the exhibit depicting the story of the universe. He talks about how this story unfolded to a great extent during his lifetime and that he had spent his career attempting to understand it, and he expresses his realization that it will be foundational for his grandchildren.[44] Peacocke presents Christianity as a tradition that is capable of embracing its past while remaining open to and incorporating this ever emerging knowledge of the world we live in that is brought to us through the empirical pursuit of science. Therefore, Peacocke's understanding of Christianity can be seen as an example of how established religions can coordinate with and contribute to a contemplation of the significance of the approximately 14-billion-year history of our creative universe from which all life, including our own, has emerged.

V. Conclusion

Only time will tell the extent to which forms of valuation and spirituality move forward to accompany this ever-expanding story that comes to us through the natural sciences. In his *A Primer for Environmental Literacy*, Golley describes the concept of connectedness as follows:

> Connectedness requires a response from us... First, we need to acknowledge the connections we make with nature and the other. When students ask me how to do this, my answer is prayer. Prayer is a private, silent statement recognizing connection. We need to express our understanding of connectedness by consciously affirming that we are part of environments, connected to them in ways we do not understand, and that we accept a responsibility for being connected to another. A simple statement of the fact of being connected is a first step toward a deeper acknowledgement of one's role and responsibility. Then, in time, the prayer can become more personal and richer with intention and meaning.[45]

I could never sum it up any better than this except to say that never has there been a more urgent time for us to recognize our physical and spiritual connectedness with all of life on Earth. What is needed is a realization that we are, as this quotation demonstrates, intimately connected to all of life, and that we cannot expect to prosper if we do not have a conservation ethic that considers the protection of nature a primary goal. This realization should be the goal of all of us, whether religious or not. However, perhaps there is a potentially unique contribution available to religious communities. In the following chapters, I will argue that a sacramental view of nature grounded in the understanding of the experience of the divine through material reality has the potential to make a significant contribution toward the protection of the Earth's threatened biodiversity as well as to enhance and broaden the sacramental tradition as it is lived out in Christian faith and worship. The etymological root of the word religion implies a binding together. The term ecology, derived from the Greek root *oikos* meaning house, can properly be understood as the study of the connectedness of the Earth's households. In my humble opinion, it is time that we act on these realizations for the good of ourselves and for all of our earthly kin.

Chapter Two

Sacrament and Sacramentality: A Eucharistic Theology of Ecological Grace

I. Introduction

According to E. O. Wilson, a proper understanding and appreciation of this "Epic of Evolution" is the key to attributing the ecological value that is necessary to protect the world's threatened biodiversity.[46] In *Biophilia*, he writes, "I will make the case that to explore and affiliate with life is a deep and complicated process in mental development. To an extent still undervalued in philosophy and religion, our existence depends on this propensity, our spirit is woven from it, hope rises on its currents." Further, he concludes: "to the degree that we come to understand other organisms, we will place a greater value on them, and on ourselves."[47] I agree with Wilson on this point, and in this chapter, I will address Wilson's reference to religion's undervaluation of our inextricable connectedness to nature by exploring the relationship between the scientific narrative of the Epic of Evolution, ecological value, and the sacramental life of the Christian church.

More specifically, I will argue that the sacramental understanding of grace present in the Christian Eucharist can serve as an effective means to perpetuate ecological value for all of life and therefore serve as a valuable contribution to the conservation of the Earth's biodiversity. Continuing the conversation begun in the previous chapter, particular attention will be focused on Wilson and Ursula Goodenough, two scientists who claim that understanding the ecological and genetic kinship of all living things will lead to the attribution of value to the ecological communities upon which we all depend for sustenance. Concurrently, by

22

incorporating the concept of a "sacramental universe" from Anglican sacramental theology, I propose that the grace that is understood to be present in the substances of the bread and wine of the Eucharist points outwards so that it can also be witnessed in all of God's ongoing Creation.[48] Therefore, sacramental grace can potentially become a primary means for the Christian community to value, revere, and consequently care for the natural or created order.

Connecting the scientific narrative of the Epic of Evolution with a religious understanding of sacramental grace will seem to many to be a bit of a stretch, but if you will bear with me for a while longer, I intend to show that not only are a sacramental understanding of Eucharistic grace and ecological value compatible but also that a sacramental approach to ecology can potentially expand the scope and effectiveness of contemporary efforts to protect life on Earth. Before moving into a discussion of how the idea of Eucharistic grace can perpetuate the ecological value that emerges from a proper understanding of the Epic of Evolution, let us first further examine the connections between scientific and religious narratives that have been recognized as present in the Epic itself.

II. A Naturalist's Revelation

I have to admit that I have always read E. O. Wilson as a deeply religious author. It is necessary to clarify here that I am not claiming that Wilson identifies himself as such. Wilson certainly makes no such claims but is instead a self-professed secular humanist. In fact, in conversations concerning the relationship between religion and science, Wilson is quite frequently accused by religious critics of being overly reductionistic in his understanding of religion. There is certainly some truth to this criticism given Wilson's claim that religion, as well as ethics, are products of human evolutionary history that served as adaptive traits contributing to the survival of our *Homo sapiens* ancestors.[49] Furthermore, he predicts that the "eventual result of the competition between the two worldviews [religion and science]...will be the secularization of the human epic and of religion itself."[50]

Yet, if one pays close enough attention, Wilson's criticism involves a rejection of a particular type of religious narrative, supernaturalistic religious narratives that contradict and claim to compete with the Epic of Evolution. However, he does not necessarily reject what might be called a religious or spiritual orientation.[51] Recognizing the importance of storytelling in human culture, he writes, "People need a sacred narrative. They must have a sense of larger purpose, in one form or other, however, intellectualized."[52] For Wilson, the traditional orienting function of religious narratives remains, but he wishes to substitute a new, naturalistic narrative that will better orient humans toward a proper understanding of our kinship with all of life.[53] The awe, beauty, and wonder traditionally associated with religious devotion is maintained but is inspired not by the supernatural but instead by a naturalistic account of the Earth's ecology.[54]

Therefore, in this sense, the Epic of Evolution, as understood by Wilson, is connected to the function of traditional religious narratives of origin and orientation and is the most proper narrative to help us address the issue of the protection of the threatened biodiversity in our contemporary context.[55] In his Pulitzer Prize winning *On Human Nature* first published in 1978, he writes that "the evolutionary epic is probably the best myth we will ever have. It can be adjusted until it comes as close to truth as the human mind is constructed to judge the truth."[56] Elsewhere, in describing the religious function of the Epic of Evolution, Wilson writes: "If the sacred narrative cannot be in the form of a religious cosmology, it will be taken from the material history of the universe and the human species. That trend is in no way debasing. The true evolutionary epic, retold as poetry, is as intrinsically ennobling as any religious epic. Material reality discovered by science already possesses more content and grandeur than all religious cosmologies combined."[57] We see here, once again, that Wilson's interpretation of the Epic represents both a rejection of and a connection to the function of traditional religious narratives.

However, I believe that the religious significance of Wilson's work is deeper than simply serving as a contemporary scientific alternative for the function of traditional religious narratives. I say this because there is evidence in aspects of Wilson's writings of a clear and profound respect for human spirituality. Furthermore, there are also indications that his work to establish a conservation ethic based on the Epic of Evolution is a continuation, albeit a reinterpretation, of the religiosity of his childhood acculturation. Describing his journey in young adulthood from supernatural theism to a complete devotion to natural history, he states: "I had no desire to purge religious feelings. They were bred in me; they suffused the wellsprings of my creative life."[58] In an even more revealing passage from his autobiography, *Naturalist*, he describes the process by which he drifted away from the Southern Baptist faith of his acculturation and his consequent reinterpretation of grace and its relation to the attribution of value:

The still faithful might say I never truly knew grace, never had it; but they would be wrong. The truth is that I found it and abandoned it. In the years following I drifted away from the church, and my attendance became desultory. My heart continued to believe in the light and the way, but increasingly in the abstract, and I looked for grace in some other setting. By the time I entered college at the age of seventeen, I was absorbed in natural history almost to the exclusion of everything else. I was enchanted with science as a means of explaining the physical world, which increasingly seemed to me to be the complete world. In essence, I still longed for grace, but rooted solidly on Earth.[59]

It is in this sense that I feel comfortable referring to Wilson as a deeply religious author. His goal is not to explain away the importance of a religious/spiritual impetus in human culture but to urge that human spirituality should be expressed in a way that recognizes nature as "vital to our physical and spiritual well-being" and that the "spiritual roots of *Homo sapiens* extend deep into the natural world through still mostly hidden channels of mental development."[60] Value or grace, to use his term, emerges from material reality. For Wilson, what emerges from the scientific narrative is a unique form of valuation that results from understanding the complex and intricately connected life on Earth. In his words, "[t]o know this world is to gain proprietary attachment to it. To know it well is to love and take responsibility for it."[61] I think it is justifiable to classify such a response as sacramental. It is to this topic that I will now turn.

III. A Sacramental Ecology of the Eucharist

The Book of Common Prayer defines the sacraments as "outward and visible signs of inward and spiritual grace, given by Christ as sure and certain means by which we can receive that grace."[62] This definition tells us two things. First, it tells us that the Christian sacramental system is inextricably linked with the life, ministry, and sacramental significance of Jesus, understood by Christians to be the Christ or "anointed one" of God. It also tells us quite clearly that, sacramentally, we experience God's grace through material reality. In the Eucharist, this grace is conveyed through the substances of water, bread, and wine. It does not take much of an imagination to expand the understanding of grace conveyed in these material substances to an acceptance that Divine grace is constantly present to us in the natural environment if we will only take the opportunity to recognize it.

In fact, such an expansion of sacramental grace is quite clearly encouraged in the Book of Common Prayer: "God does not limit God's self to these rites; they are patterns of countless ways by which God uses material things to reach out to us."[63] In other words, when we receive the Eucharist as a part of Christian sacramental liturgy, it is not intended as an escape from the world but as spiritual nourishment so that we may be sent back into the world to recognize the grace that is potentially present in all of God's ongoing Creation. We are released from the Eucharistic rite to experience Divine grace in our day to day lives in our local environments, that is, in nature. Consider the words from the post communion prayer in the Book of Common Prayer: "[Y]ou have fed us with spiritual food in the Sacrament of his Body and Blood. Send us now into the world in peace, and grant us strength and courage to love and serve you with gladness and singleness of heart; through Christ our Lord. Amen."[64] If we experience grace in the material substances of the bread, wine, and water present in the Christian sacraments, this grace is not confined within the boundaries of an individual liturgy or the walls of a church community but instead informs those who participate in these sacraments that God's grace can be revealed to us through anything or anyone we may encounter in our Earthly lives. Because value is necessarily applied to any means through which grace is potentially conveyed in the world, the implications of such a view for the attribution of ecological value are clear.

A prominent example of such a view in Anglican sacramental theology can be found in William Temple's Gifford Lectures where he refers to the "sacramental universe" in which we live out our lives.[65] In other words, if God is the source, center, and end of all material reality, then Divine grace is present to us in all that exists.[66] As I established previously, Christian sacramentalism is grounded in material reality. According to Temple, Christianity "is the most avowedly materialist of all the great religions."[67] Therefore, a valuation of the material through the Christian commitment to an incarnational, sacramental view of Divine grace allows this valuation to be extended outward in a manner in which all that exists is potentially sacramental.

What we have here is a distinction between the unique sacraments of the Christian church and a more general form of sacramentality toward which they point. In *A Guide to the Sacraments*, John Macquarrie describes this extension of the sacramental system to a more generalized sacramentality: "Perhaps the goal of all sacramentality and sacramental theology is to make the things of this world so transparent that in them and through them we know God's presence and activity in our very midst, and so experience his grace." According to Macquarrie, this "general notion of sacramentality ... is not exclusively confined to Christianity but is found in many religions and philosophies."[68] The significance of such an understanding of sacramentality for the attribution of ecological value is that the conveyers of sacramental grace are no longer seen as "'mere' things, but as bearers of meaning, value and potentiality, as messages from the ultimate mystery we call God."[69] It is through the acceptance of the broader sacramentality of a sacramental universe where the Christian concept of sacramental grace is seamlessly brought into a relationship with the ecological value inspired though a proper interpretation of the evolutionary epic. In both understandings, what emerges from the inherent connectedness of ecological communities is greater than what can be predicated simply from a knowledge of the biological component parts of these communities.[70] Regardless of whether it is explicitly attributed with a connection with the Divine, the beautiful mystery of life on Earth inspires a sense of grace and therefore value for all of the natural, created order.

An excellent example of this relationship between

sacramentality and the Epic of Evolution is demonstrated in Ursula Goodenough's *The Sacred Depths of Nature*. Like Wilson, Goodenough believes that the Epic of Evolution is the best orienting narrative to inspire an effective ecological ethic in humans.[71] However, she unequivocally refers to the value that emerges from her understanding of the Epic as a form of religious naturalism. As a result, she is even more explicit than Wilson in her association with religion in describing our relationship with nature. In her words, there is a sense of gratitude and reverence that flows from the "Mystery of why there is anything at all, rather than nothing."[72] Goodenough describes her understanding of religious reverence in relation to natural value as follows: "Reverence is the religious emotion elicited when we perceive the sacred. We are called to revere the whole enterprise of planetary existence, the whole and all of its myriad parts as they catalyze and secrete and replicate and mutate and evolve."[73] Furthermore, she continues: "If we can revere how things are, and can find a way to express gratitude for our existence, then we should be able to figure out, with a great deal of work and good will, how to share the Earth with one another and with other creatures, how to restore and preserve its elegance and grace, and how to commit ourselves to love and joy and laughter and hope."[74]

Goodenough is advocating a form of naturalistic grace that mirrors Wilson's call for a valuation of nature. For both Wilson and Goodenough, value emerges from material reality, through an understanding of the natural history of life from which we emerged, and is the source of our physical as well as our spiritual sustenance. This view is perfectly consistent with the broader notion of sacramentality that potentially flows from Christian sacramental tradition. However, if you will recall the Book of Common Prayer's definition of sacrament quoted above, there is also a tension between the uniqueness of a Christian sacramental rite, which has its origin in the witness to the life of

Jesus and is rooted in the history of Christian tradition, and the ecological value toward which it potentially points. It is now necessary to address this potential discontinuity by returning to a more detailed discussion of the ecological significance of the sacramental rite of the Eucharist.

If one is going to assess the ecological significance of the Christian sacraments, the Eucharist is a good place to start. First, of the seven formal sacraments recognized in Christian tradition, the Eucharist is the one that is observed most frequently. As Macquarrie points out, the Eucharist is "the sacrament of maturity, which the communicant will continue to receive for the rest of his or her life and which will promote spiritual growth."[75] We have examined how an understanding of Eucharistic grace in the substances of water, bread, and wine can be expanded to include a broader sacramentality for the entire natural environment. However, if Christian sacramental worship is going to make a significant contribution to the attribution of ecological value, the ecological value attributed must be considered inseparably related to the Christian tradition of which it is a part. As a result, we must move beyond simply focusing on the acceptance of the basic materiality of the substance of the Eucharist and examine, in a deeper way, the theological and ritual significance of the sacrament itself. If a connection to the evolutionary epic is considered to be shoehorned into or simply a nice addendum to the sacramental tradition instead of emerging from the very heart of the tradition itself, it will not resonate and will therefore fall short of the potential I am claiming for it.

The Eucharist, perhaps more than any of the other sacraments of the church, represents the potential and tension between the specific, formal sacraments of the church and the broader sacramentality that can potentially lead to a recognition of Divine grace in a sacramental universe. This is the case because the entire Christian theological narrative, the Alpha, Chi,

Omega of Christian tradition, is contained in the sacramental worship of the Eucharist. Our scriptural tradition begins with a poetic story of Divine Creation in which we are told that all of the created order is endowed with goodness as it is spoken into existence by the Spirit of God.[76] As Christians, we seek to understand the mystery of the incarnation of this Divine Word, the source of all life, through whom all things come into being.[77] And, we look forward in hope toward an eschatological fulfillment where Life will ultimately emerge from suffering and death.[78] These theological concepts lie at the heart of Christian sacramental tradition and undergird the Eucharistic liturgy.[79] They are also undeniably ecological in nature. Therefore, the Eucharist orients its participants in the present while allowing us to simultaneously look inward, backward, and forward to discern how the theological concepts of creation, incarnation, and resurrection, which are inherent to the Eucharistic meal and integral to the eschatological hope of Christian tradition, project outward to correspond to the presence of Divine grace in all of material reality.[80]

In relation to the evolutionary epic, this naturalistic interpretation of the Eucharist can be seen as a narrative within a narrative. The Epic of Evolution as described by Wilson and Goodenough is a universal narrative that unites us all, genetically and ecologically, whether we choose to accept this or not. In our pluralistic cultural context, we must recognize that the Christian narrative as represented in the reiteration of the Eucharistic meal is not universal. It arose within the last few thousand years and is a part of a particular human history connected to the larger history of our species, *Homo sapiens,* that spans 100,000–200,000 years. In other words, we can say that nature is the source for all of the sacraments and therefore necessarily preceded any particular sacramental tradition.

However, there is also a deeper connection between Christian sacramental worship and the 14-billion-year cosmic history of our universe from which life emerged. Although the Eucharist is contained within the larger sacramental ecology of the history of life on Earth and the cosmic history of the universe, it is through participation in the Eucharistic liturgy that Christian worshipers can be ritually made aware of the grace that is present to be experienced in a sacramental universe. In other words, it is the reiteration of sacramental worship that has the greatest potential to point toward an awareness of and appreciation for a broader sense of sacramentality. While the Book of Common Prayer's definition of sacrament as an outward and visible sign of an inward and spiritual grace supports a broader sacramentality, it is the unique sacraments of the church which point us outward to worship sacramentally in all of God's ongoing Creation.[81]

Furthermore, Christian tradition has a significant cosmic perspective through the theological understanding that God's grace is incarnate sacramentally through the creative action of the Divine Word in our sacramental universe. Therefore, the ecological value attributed through the Eucharist can be understood as inherent in instead of extraneous to the Christian tradition from which it emerges. The very meaning of tradition implies that our faith must be applied anew to shape and shape us in the cultures we find ourselves in in our contemporary context. Therefore, we need only to reenvision, as opposed to reinvent, our Eucharistic theology to seamlessly connect the concept of sacramental grace to the ecological value that emerges from a proper understanding of the evolutionary history of life on Earth.

Before concluding this chapter, it is necessary to address in more detail a couple of additional issues that are pertinent to this topic: First, it is necessary to address the distinction between naturalism and supernaturalism that is always in the background of any discussion of the relationship between theistic religion and science. Van A. Harvey defines naturalism as follows: "Naturalism means quite generally that view which denies the existence of any reality transcending nature. It stands opposed, therefore, to any kind of supernaturalism, if by the latter is meant any deity or being apart from nature."[82] In this chapter, I have applied the term naturalism to both Christian sacramentalism and the Epic of Evolution, but I want to offer a slight revision of Harvey's definition by saying that the rejection of supernaturalism, an approach which categorically conflicts with a naturalistic perspective, does not preclude an acceptance of mystery, spirituality, value, and grace. Nor, I would argue, does it necessarily reject the possibility of a certain form of theism since, from a sacramental point of view, the Divine is understood to be inseparable and not apart from nature.

Both Wilson and Goodenough's interpretation of the Epic of Evolution is explicitly non-theistic yet is deeply imbued with a sense of mystery and value. Consider again, for example, Goodenough's "confession of faith" in religious naturalism cited in the previous chapter:

> And so, I profess my Faith. For me, the existence of all this complexity and awareness and intent and beauty, and my ability to apprehend it, serves as the ultimate meaning and the ultimate value. The continuation of life reaches around, grabs its own tail, and forms a sacred circle that requires no further justification, no Creator, no superordinate meaning of meaning, no purpose other than that the continuation continue until the sun collapses or the final meteor collides. I confess a credo of continuation.[83]

This is an example of the type of sacramentality that I have said can potentially flow from but is not synonymous with a Christian sacramental approach.

However, one can clearly see a commitment to unite the natural and spiritual while avoiding the supernatural from the perspective of Christian sacramental theology as well:

Macquarrie states this clearly at the outset of his *A Guide to the Sacraments*: "My aim is to maintain the genuine mystery of the sacraments as a means by which divine grace is mediated to us in this world of space and time and matter, but at the same time to get away from all magical and superstitious ideas about them."[84] In their *Introduction to Theology*, Owen C. Thomas and Ellen K. Wondra support such a view with their explanation of the sacramental relationship between the natural and the spiritual: "In the Christian sacramental view, the spiritual expresses itself by acting in and through the material and not by ignoring or suppressing it. And the material acts as the vehicle, the expression, and the instrument of the spiritual."[85] Understood properly, the Eucharist exhibits a strong commitment to a form of naturalism that is infused with spiritual grace. From what we have seen here, I think we could say that is a view that is also potentially true of the broader form of sacramentality present in the Epic of Evolution.

One of the beautiful characteristics of the Epic of Evolution is that it can be interpreted either theistically or non-theistically. In a short article titled "Ultimacy," Goodenough describes a conversation she had with theologian Belden Lane after the publication of *The Sacred Depths of Nature*. Before their meeting, Goodenough expresses some anxiety that Lane was going to critique her claim to be a non-theistic religious naturalist. Instead, he was more interested in making sure that he had properly understood the scientific concepts Goodenough had outlined in the text. She describes their conversation as follows:

Every time he'd really get something, see the world in a whole new way, he'd throw back his head with a huge smile and say something like "Isn't it astonishing what God has done?" And I'd say "Isn't it astonishing?" As we became aware of this interplay, we also became deeply excited about its meaning. In the end, the God part was added on to our shared experience of wonder. Belden could add it, I couldn't, and it didn't matter to either of us, didn't matter that that part was different. The point was that we were rejoicing in the story in exactly the same way.[86]

In other words, there is a miracle in the emergence and complexity and beauty of life, and this can be perceived theistically or non-theistically while maintaining a complete commitment to naturalism.[87] For those of us who are theists, I do not think that it is difficult to accept that the grace of God is present to all living things whether we realize it or not and also that this grace does not depend on human recognition for it to be efficacious.

Additionally, thus far, the grace and value that I have discussed as being attributed to nature has involved, for the most part, a sense of awe, beauty, celebration, and wonder associated with our realization of the deep connectedness inherent in life on Earth. However, while love and altruism emerge from the evolutionary epic, so do suffering and death, and we must recognize this if such an understanding of grace and value is going to resonate as a spiritually satisfying form of religion. In other words, to paraphrase a response from a parishioner at an Adult Education Forum where I spoke on a related topic, "What do you do about black holes and hurricanes?" While there are never completely satisfying answers to the issues surrounding suffering and death, both the Epic and Evolution and the sacrament of the Eucharist provide a credible response. Concerning the issue of meaning and death, Goodenough writes,

Sex without death gets you single-celled algae and fungi; sex with a mortal soma gets you the rest of the eukaryotic creatures. Death is the price paid to have trees and clams and birds and grasshoppers, and death is the price paid to have human consciousness, to be aware of all that shimmering awareness and all that love. My somatic life is the wondrous gift wrought by my forthcoming death.[88]

Participation in the Eucharist can also offer us a means to deal with all of the reality of human existence. In his *Worship As Theology: Foretaste of Glory Divine*, Don E. Saliers describes Christian liturgical worship as a means to express thanksgiving and gratitude for the connections we share as a part of the lives we lead in God's creation.[89] However, he is quick to point out that "praise and thanksgiving grow empty when the truth about human rage and over suffering and injustice is never uttered" and that "lamentation is necessary to keep praise and thanksgiving from evading the real."[90] As stated earlier, the Eucharist does not offer an escape from the world. Consequently, it also does not offer us an escape from the realities of the lives we live in the world. Eucharist means thanksgiving, but the grace received in the Eucharist is a thanksgiving offered in the context of the reality of our lives as an attempt to find meaning and significance in our joys as well as our sorrows.

IV. Conclusion

Schubert Ogden maintains that all Christian theological claims must abide by the criteria of appropriateness and credibility.[91] According to Ogden, Christian theology must be appropriate in the sense that it simultaneously accepts a connection to the tradition of which it is inextricably a part as well as credible to the contemporary context in which we live our lives. It has been my goal in this chapter to abide by these criteria. My hope is that what I have said here would at least be considered plausible if not accepted by non-religious scientists such as Wilson and sacramental traditionalists alike. The Epic of Evolution compels us to look backward to our natural history for the purpose of understanding where we came from and who we are in our contemporary context so that we may value and protect the Earth's ecology as we go forward. The Eucharistic sacrament, while firmly rooted in Christian tradition, has the potential to significantly contribute to this backward and forward perspective by orienting us toward the recognition of sacramental grace present in the ongoing evolutionary epic. From this perspective, the Christian sacramental tradition can be understood as distinct but inseparably related to a broader understanding of sacramentality in which God's grace can be potentially witnessed, understood, and valued in all aspects of the natural world. As we come to the Eucharistic table, we humbly embrace life in all of its uncertainty, joy, sorrow, complexity, and beauty by fully immersing ourselves in sacramental worship so that we may come to revere and protect God's ongoing Creation, what Wilson refers to as "Living Nature," the source of all grace and value.[92] Recognizing the power of religious and scientific narratives in our time, Wilson claims that, "[i]f religion and science could be united on the common ground of biological conservation, the problem would soon be solved."[93] I propose that a deeper exploration of the ecological significance of sacramental theology is a step in the right direction.

Chapter Three

A Beautiful Mystery: Divine Eucharistic Presence, the Epic of Evolution, and the Love of Life on Earth

I. Introduction

In Chapter Two, I used the distinction between sacrament and sacramentality to propose that the Christian sacrament of the Eucharist is distinct from but inseparably related to a broader sacramentality. In brief, an understanding of the grace conveyed through the material substances of water, bread and wine in the Eucharist can be expanded to include the presence of grace in all of material reality establishing what I refer to as a "sacramental ecology" of life on Earth. Furthermore, while Eucharistic worship is contained within an understanding of a broader "sacramental universe," I argue that, for Christians, it is the practice of the sacrament itself which orients the worshiping community to a deeper sense of the existence of grace, and therefore value, in the natural environment.[94]

In this chapter, I will engage in a more detailed study of the potential continuities and discontinuities between a historical understanding and contemporary practice of the Eucharist and the extended notion of a sacramental universe. I will do this through an examination of the concept of real presence and the related issues of sacrifice and mystery associated with the Eucharistic sacrament. Entailed in this discussion of the ecological significance of real presence will be an assessment of Edward Schillebeeckx's understanding of Christ as "primordial sacrament" and an evaluation of the ways in which the sacrificial language of Eucharistic worship potentially creates both creative possibilities and conflicts within this conversation. Also involved will be an examination of the potential for the language of mystery to uncover an intimate connection between a deep commitment to the historical tradition of Eucharistic sacramental worship and the necessity of speaking to issues of ecological crises in our contemporary context. In brief, I will argue that, for Christians, the acceptance of the presence of Christ in the Eucharist, instead of a stumbling block, can be the key that opens us up to a broader sense of sacramentality wherein participation in the Eucharist can honestly address the issue of connections between sacramental grace and the ecological value related to the narrative of the Epic of Evolution.

II. Eucharistic Sacrifice of Life, Love, and Community

If one is to successfully argue for a Eucharistic theology of ecological grace, a more engaged inquiry into the significance of the Eucharist itself is necessary since, in the attempt to apply Christian tradition to contemporary issues of ecological concern, there is a temptation to simply highlight the materiality of the Eucharistic substances without going deeper into the significance of Jesus for the sacrament itself. Certainly, as I alluded to above, there are clear continuities between the grace conveyed through material reality in the Eucharist and the attribution of ecological value that coincides with an understanding of the connectedness inherent in nature. However, simply emphasizing these compatibilities while diverting attention from any potential problems would not demonstrate a proper respect for the tradition from which contemporary sacramental worship emerged and to which it is inextricably linked. Furthermore, any Christian theology attempting, whether consciously or unconsciously, to downplay the centrality of Jesus in order to maintain a supposed coherence with a contemporary context has internally provided the critique for undermining its legitimacy. In other words, if there are discontinuities between an understanding of the application of sacramental grace in the Eucharist and the attribution of ecological value, we need to stare them right in the face and not divert our attention for the sake of convenience or upholding an argument we hope to be true.

With this in mind, a good place to begin such a deeper inquiry is with an examination of the language of Eucharistic sacrifice, a concept that is integral to the historical understanding of the Eucharist but also one that can be highly problematic when an attempt is made to apply Christian tradition to a broader cultural and ecological context. This is particularly the case when this sacrificial language is understood as a propitiatory sacrifice of atonement for the forgiveness of sins. For example, in *A Guide to the Sacraments*, John Macquarrie writes that it "is a pity that religious sacrifice is closely associated in popular thinking with killing and shedding of blood.... The modern mind turns away from such an idea in horror."[95] Voicing a similar sentiment, Bruce Morrill makes clear the problematic nature of attempting to maintain, in our contemporary context, an interpretation of Jesus' death as a propitiatory sacrifice for the atonement of human sins: "The impotence of the conventional Christian myth of sacrifice and atonement at the dawn of the new millennium is evident in the 'mainstream' churches' struggles for effective influence upon society — locally, nationally, or now globally — and in the lives of individuals."[96] These are serious criticisms which must be addressed, and given the difficulties posed by such interpretations for connecting this primary rite of Christian sacramental worship to issues of contemporary ecological concern, it is certainly tempting to simply advocate for an avoidance of sacrificial language altogether.

However, given what was stated above about the necessity of engaging with potential discontinuities if one is to be true to Christian tradition while attempting to apply that tradition in a contemporary context, this is not really an option since sacrificial language has been at the heart of Eucharistic worship from the very emergent stages of Christianity. In their history of the

Eucharistic liturgy, Paul F. Bradshaw and Maxwell E. Johnson claim "that there is no question but that the Eucharist was widely understood theologically as the Church's 'sacrifice' and, as such, the burden of proof to the contrary has always been (and remains) on those who wish somehow to deny this interpretation and who seek to avoid using sacrificial terminology altogether in their Eucharistic practice and theology."[97] Therefore, what is needed is not a complete jettisoning of the use of sacrificial language but instead a more thorough examination of the development of this language in order to avoid allowing a particular interpretation to, in Macquarrie's words, "prejudice us against a better understanding of sacrifice."[98] In order to do this, we must take into consideration various ways that sacrificial language has been used throughout Christian history in relation to Eucharistic practice so that our re-appropriation of the term in the present can be both consistent with Christian tradition and credible to the wider cultural and ecological setting in which it is being applied.[99]

First, the development of the sacrificial language of the Eucharistic sacrament is deeply grounded in the rituals of the cultural settings from which it emerged, and when one takes a closer look, what becomes clearer is a variety of interpretations as opposed to a unified understanding of the meaning and use of the terminology of sacrifice.[100] Connecting the development of the Eucharist with the Jewish communion sacrifice, Morrill writes that "Biblical Judaism had a number of different practices we gloss under the generic term *sacrifice*, including but hardly limited to expiatory rituals in reparation for sin. The common thread running through them is best grasped in terms of offering, an act of offering that renders a response or return to God, an offering that unites the people with God."[101] In their assessment of early Christian meals, Bradshaw and Johnson point to early Christian documents such as the *Didache*, one of the earliest dated catechetical texts of the Church, that "view the Eucharistic elements as life-giving and spiritually nourishing rather than in sacrificial terms."[102] Furthermore, they claim that the Eucharistic prayers of thanksgiving were accepted by early Christians as a substitute for temple sacrifice and "were understood as the primary sacrifice that was offered in the Eucharist" with the *Didache* appearing to serve as "the earliest explicit example of this."[103] What these examples demonstrate is that the sacrificial language appearing in these early documents of Christian life and worship does not present sacrifice in exclusively propitiatory terms. Instead, the sacrifice of the Eucharist points more comprehensively to a broader sense of union with God and thanksgiving for the life sustaining and nourishing gifts of Creation.[104]

Of course, the sacrificial language of the New Testament Last Supper narratives, in which Jesus relates his own body and blood to the Eucharistic elements of bread and wine, is also a part of this early history. Accepting that the Last Supper accounts are examples of a Jewish Passover meal which involved the understanding that "the blood of the sacrificed lambs procured deliverance for the Israelites," Macquarrie describes this connection as follows:

> It was surely natural to see the new rite which arose out of the Last Supper of Jesus with the disciples as the equivalent of the old Passover, the sacrifice of a new covenant replacing the old. Jesus' own death very soon came to be regarded in sacrificial terms. When he said at that last meal, "This is my body" and "This is my blood of the covenant which is poured out for many" (Mark 12:22, 24), this could hardly fail to imply that here was a new Passover bringing deliverance, a Passover in which Jesus is himself the paschal lamb.[105]

However, Bradshaw and Johnson point out that we should be careful in uncritically accepting the view that the Gospel narratives of the Last Supper provide a clear record of the "institution" of the primary understanding of early Christian Eucharistic practice.[106] In fact, they claim that Jesus' speaking over the bread and wine in sacrificial language in the Last Supper narratives was likely a minority tradition in the early Church perhaps introduced initially by the writings of Paul. They write:

> Thus, the Last Supper version of the eucharistic sayings of Jesus may not have been as dominant in first-century Christianity as the existence of four accounts of it in the New Testament books may tempt us to suppose. Paul in 1 Corinthians 11 may even have been the originator of the tradition of associating Jesus' sayings about the bread and cup being his body and blood with the Last Supper and consequently giving them a sacrificial interpretation, which was later taken up in Mark's gospel and through that in Matthew and Luke.[107]

This does not mean that this particular narrative should be ignored or suppressed but only that it should be recognized that it existed in the context of a variety of understandings of the Eucharistic sacrifice. In fact, given the early presence and later predominance in Christian history of the tradition of Jesus' "institution" of the Eucharist at the Last Supper, it would be irresponsible to simply cast it aside as if we could easily dispense with its influence.

Furthermore, the Last Supper narratives need not be interpreted exclusively in terms of a bloody, propitiatory sacrifice for the forgiveness of sins. In fact, it would be anachronistic to read such a clear understanding of the bread and wine of the Eucharist as akin to Christ's bodily sacrifice into the earliest centuries of Christian history since this view developed gradually during the first millennium of Christian history and did not begin to move toward any type of theologically explicit doctrinal understanding until centuries later.[108] For example, Bradshaw and Johnson claim "that in the early centuries of Christianity there was a general acceptance that Christ was in some way present in the Eucharistic bread and wine—that they were his body and blood. Exactly in what sense this was so was apparently not explored, and it did not become a topic of philosophical debate among Western theologians until the ninth century."[109] Such an understanding not only opens us up to the possibility of recognizing a variety of interpretations of the "institution narratives" in early Christianity but also encourages us to reassess the significance and applicability of the language of sacrifice for us in the lives we lead in the present.

Bernard Cooke relates the sacrifice of Christ in the Eucharist to the self-giving action of Jesus in which we are called to participate. In his words, this "means that the risen Christ is giving himself in new life to his friends. This self-giving by the risen Lord is his continuing action of 'offering sacrifice.' And the corollary of this is that Christians' action of 'offering sacrifice' consists in their loving self-gift to their fellow humans."[110] Therefore, according to Cooke, "what the eucharist celebrates is that the entire life of these Christians, if lived out in loving concern for and genuine self-gift to their fellow humans, is a living sacrifice."[111] The mention here of self-giving and life is very important as it opens us up to a life of loving relationship with others, which, as Cooke points out, includes our fellow humans, but for the purpose of my argument, I would like to insist that this self-giving sacrifice can be extended to include all of God's ongoing Creation.

It is fortunate for those of us who are arguing for the applicability of sacrificial language in our contemporary context that Cooke is not alone in this sentiment. For example, Morrill offers a position supportive of Cooke's when he relates the early Christian term "spiritual sacrifices" "to believers' ongoing offering of their very lives in service to others." "The church," he continues, "shares in its members the deep and abiding knowledge of the mystery of God as self-emptying love for humanity in celebrating the Eucharist."[112] Macquarrie references Hugh Blenkin's claim "that the fundamental purpose of sacrifice is the bestowal of life. This statement," he writes, "puts life rather than death at the centre of sacrifice. This is important when we think of the sacrifice or self-offering of Jesus Christ, whether on Calvary or in relation to the eucharist. It is something affirmative for the human race."[113] In this same discussion, he adds the following: "In any discussion of eucharistic sacrifice, we must put away any ideas which think of atonement as a negative transaction designed to save us *from* some unhappy fate, and see it in affirmative terms as making human beings 'at one' with God, bringing them new life from God."[114] Such a life-affirming understanding of sacrificial language allows us to avoid some of the negative connotations of the term sacrifice that are so off putting in our modern context. While the interpretation of the Eucharist as propitiatory sacrifice for the atonement of sins is still with us and persists strongly in some circles of the Church, there are other narratives at our disposal that can serve as alternatives to those that no longer seem applicable in our current cultural environments. By embracing a life-affirming narrative of service in the world, our participation in the Eucharist becomes an impetus for us to emulate Jesus by entering into the sacrificial, self-giving life characterized by our intimate connection with our fellow worshipers, the wider cultural communities in which we exist, and all life that exists and continues to emerge from its creative, divine source. Sacrifice, understood in this way, allows us to foster an awareness that all of life is intimately related and sustained by the loving presence of God and that we consequently have a responsibility to value and protect the sacramental ecology through which grace, and therefore value, flows.

III. Divine Presence and Mystery in Sacramental Grace and Ecological Value

I now want to turn to the concept of real divine presence in the Eucharist, a concept that undergirds all of the issues discussed in this paper. Real presence in the Eucharist has been interpreted rather broadly; however, for my purposes in this chapter, I will focus on the understanding of real presence in the substances of the Eucharistic gifts of bread and wine, which entails an examination of the doctrine of transubstantiation.[115] Later in this section, I will return to a discussion of how our relationship with the real presence of Christ in the Eucharist can make us aware of our deep connections to God and to our cultural and ecological communities, but I want to begin with a point of discontinuity related to the unhelpful interpretations of sacrifice discussed in the previous section.

Transubstantiation has long been a stumbling block for Western Christianity, one that contributed to well-defined battle lines during the Reformation and one that is still often highly contentious in current theological discourse. This is due in large part to the fact that the doctrine of transubstantiation was the culmination of the increased emphasis, begun in the ninth century, on the understanding of the gifts of the Eucharistic bread and wine as being transformed into the sacrificial body and blood of Jesus as conveyers of divine grace.[116] It was accepted as doctrine at the Fourth Lateran Council (1215) and has been continuously confirmed by the official teaching of the Catholic Church to the present. Contemporary criticism of transubstantiation frequently focuses on Thomas Aquinas' use of the Aristotelian categories of "substance" and "accident" in his development of the doctrine later in the thirteenth century to describe the change of substance from the gifts of bread and wine to the body and blood of Christ while retaining the "accidental" properties of the former. In the space that I have here, I do not intend to provide either a justification for or refutation of the doctrine of transubstantiation or extensively outline the various ways in which contemporary theologians have attempted to mollify its interpretation with modified theologies of real presence.[117] Instead, I want to provide some perspective on what the doctrine of transubstantiation was intended to achieve and how an understanding of real presence in our contemporary context can be applicable to a theology of sacramental ecology that is necessarily predicated on a scientific perspective of the evolutionary and ecological connectedness of life on Earth.

The problematic nature of grounding a contemporary theology of real presence in the Aristotelian metaphysical concepts of "substance" and "accident" is widely accepted in contemporary theological discourse. However, to dismiss the reality of real presence in the Eucharist along with outdated metaphysical concepts associated with transubstantiation risks limiting a deeper understanding of the development of the concept of real presence in Christian history as well as the significance that such a doctrine potentially has when lived out in the world by the Christian community. For example, referencing the importance of recognizing the real presence of Christ in the Eucharist, David Brown defends Aquinas claiming that he "sought to defend that basic conception but in a way that excluded crude physical consumption."[118] Such a corrective defense was surely needed in Aquinas' time to counter the prevalence of a literalist interpretation of the consumption of the body and blood of Christ at the Eucharistic meal.[119] For Brown, what is essential is that we continue to identify with the bodily presence in the Eucharist since we encounter Eucharistic grace through material reality, both in terms of the substances of bread and wine but also in relation to our own bodies that take in these gifts with the faithful confidence that God's saving grace is mediated in some mysterious way through them. Our recognition of the bodily kinship that all life shares with Jesus is something that Brown fears we have failed to properly emphasize in our contemporary theological conversations. He writes:

> It is only really in the modern world that understanding of Christ's presence has moved primarily towards conceiving of it in terms of a presence within the gathered community or else as some sort of rarefied personal presence, essentially no different from the ubiquity of divinity. Transubstantiation is, admittedly, by any reckoning an implausible use of Aristotelian metaphysics. It did, however, have the merit that it thereby preserved some sense of it being important that we relate to Christ as having had and continuing to have a bodily identity like our own.[120]

Therefore, this is not simply a reiteration of the traditional doctrine of transubstantiation but a commitment to the significance of the real presence of Christ in the Eucharist in our current sacramental worship. The theological concept of transubstantiation is still useful not in terms of defending its doctrinal formulation but in the sense, according to Macquarrie, that it "has come to stand for the view that there is in the eucharist a real abiding presence of Christ as against any view that denies this."[121]

Brown's insistence that we recognize the bodily presence of Christ is important not only because it affirms the goodness of the natural order but also because it asserts that God relates to us immanently in a sacramental and incarnational way through material reality.[122] Like sacrifice, the notion of real presence allows us to draw closer to God through our association with Jesus. According to Brown, the "divine nature in Christ renders his body incorruptible and so through association with that body our own too could achieve a similar status."[123] In a similar statement, he writes that "Christ's humanity is envisaged as coming close in order to create Christ-like beings in their own distinctive context."[124] By identifying with the body of Christ as real presence in the Eucharist, we can cultivate the understanding that God is still with us making the divine presence known in the lives we are living in our necessarily ecological context. In brief, our imaginative association with Christ's bodily presence strengthens our sacramental connection to the loving grace of God that is ever available to us if we will only take the time to foster an awareness of its presence.[125]

Of course, locating the real divine presence in the Eucharist is not an empirical proposition. Instead, it is an orientation to life, a life that can be understood to be infused with value, meaning, and purpose in a sacramental universe. Brown describes this as follows:

> To state the obvious, whatever Christ's present body is like, it cannot be literally material, as though with sufficient progress in science we might one day be able to reach where it is now. Its nature has somehow to be reconciled with the fact that heaven, God's dwelling place, is a non-material reality and indeed omnipresent, just as God is ... Yet none of this should be taken to indicate the abandonment of any notion of some degree of equivalence to material reality."[126]

Such an understanding is connected with the perspective that the grace conveyed through the Eucharist is, in fact, a mystery. Therefore, Brown's understanding of the bodily presence of Christ with which we identify in the Eucharist is not subject to empirical verification but is instead a mysterious presence that potentially points us toward an orientation that we, as embodied creatures, receive the grace of God through the substances of the world in which we exist and not through an ethereal or supernatural reality.

This may seem to place the understanding of real Eucharistic presence at odds with a scientific worldview. However, I would argue that the same sense of mystery that connects us to a larger presence of grace in the world through our participation in the Eucharist is the same sense that helps us value our kinship with all of life on Earth through an awareness of the Epic of Evolution. Consider Morrill's description of the place of mystery in the Eucharist:

> The word *mystery* ... is not meant to hinder believers' use of reason and imagination as they seek a greater appreciation and joy in celebrating the Eucharist. Rather, to speak of the Eucharist as mystery is to acknowledge at the outset the complexity of our inquiry, and this not as a forbidding caution but a promising invitation. In fact, "mystery" was the preferred term of the earliest Christians for referring not only to the Eucharist and baptism but to all concrete ways in which they experienced God entering into and shaping their lives in Christ.[127]

An acceptance of mystery of this kind is not a willful ignorance of scientific theory but is instead a profound respect for and faith in the source and sustenance of the lives we are blessed to live, a knowledge of which, we have to admit, is not completely knowable from our human perspective.

To further this point, it is instructive to compare this with the explanation of mystery from Bron Taylor who accepts the evolutionary and ecological history of life on Earth as the primary source of religious inspiration. Referencing environmentalist Loren Eiseley, he writes:

With Loren Eiseley, I am convinced that the theory of evolution is the best explanation for the beauty, diversity, and fecundity of the biosphere. I also agree with him that nothing in the world fully explains the world. As he puts it, "I am an evolutionist ... [but] in the world there is nothing to explain the world. Nothing to explain the necessity of life, nothing to explain the hunger of the elements to become life, nothing to explain why the stolid realm of rock and soil and mineral should diversify itself into beauty, terror, and uncertainty." This humble admission captures, I think, the idea that the universe is a Great Mystery.[128]

A willingness to accept a sense of mystery in life demonstrates a humility that is often lacking in both religious and scientific inquiry.[129] By accepting the real presence of the divine, incarnate in Christ in the Eucharist, we are, in a sense, opening ourselves to the broader mysteries of life that surround us, which, when properly understood, can also reflect to us the saving grace of God through an understanding of ecological grace in a sacramental universe. It is to a more detailed discussion of the potential for the real presence of the Christ in the Eucharist to connect to the ecological value associated with the evolutionary and cosmic history of life that I now turn.

IV. Christ, the Primordial Sacrament in a Sacramental Universe

Up to this point, I have only alluded, here and there, to how the acceptance of the real presence of Christ may point toward a broader sacramentality and a connection with the ecological grace associated with the life that emerges from the Epic of Evolution. In this last full section of this chapter, I want to take a closer look at how the mysterious bodily presence of Christ in the Eucharist can potentially connect the sacramental grace recognized in the formal ritual worship of the church with the larger sacramental universe in which it exists. I will begin with Edward Schillebeeckx's notion of Christ as the "primordial sacrament."

In the early 1960s, Edward Schillebeeckx published *Christ, the Sacrament of the Encounter with God* in which he argues that "the sacraments are the properly human mode of encounter with God" and, furthermore, that "Jesus, as the personal visible realization of the divine grace of redemption, is *the* sacrament, the primordial sacrament."[130] For Schillebeeckx, the sacraments continue the promise of the incarnation in that they serve as "the face of redemption turned visibly towards us, so that in them we are truly able to encounter the living Christ."[131] Consequently, because God is Emmanuel, "God with us" in an incarnational way through the sacraments, he claims that a "permanent sacramentality is thus an intrinsic requirement of the Christian religion."[132]

The Eucharist, in particular, serves as the material expression of Christ's bodily presence in the world. Schillebeeckx describes the primordial sacrament of Christ as a stone thrown into a pond with the ripples flowing outward in concentric circles of grace from its central point of connection with the Eucharist serving as the central sacramental activity from which grace flows: "The sacrament of the Eucharist is situated at the heart of this central point—the Eucharist is the focal point of Christ's real presence among us. Around this focal point can be seen the first radiant lights—the other six sacraments."[133] He adds that these "sacramental ripples ... continue to spread still further, though they gradually become less and less clearly defined—at this stage they are the sacramentals."[134] In other words, the real presence of Christ in the Eucharist extends beyond the formal practice of the sacrament itself and into the world with an emanating grace that is the source of a broader sacramentality.[135]

In *Hymn of the Universe*, the Jesuit paleontologist Pierre Teilhard de Chardin offers a vivid demonstration of this idea.

He relates a story in which, while observing the host, it began "gradually spreading out like a spot of oil but of course much more swiftly and luminously."[136] Continuing, he states that "through the mysterious expansion of the host the whole world had become incandescent, had itself become like a single giant host."[137] In this example, it is the host itself as the physical embodiment of the presence of Christ on Earth that reaches out to touch the universe from which all life has emerged bringing us with it into a greater realization of the immensity of divine creativity. Reflecting upon this experience, Teilhard de Chardin writes:

[M]y mind awoke to a new and higher vision of things. I began to realize vaguely that the multiplicity of evolutions into which the world-process seems to us to be split up is in fact fundamentally the working out of one single great mystery; and this first glimpse of light caused me ... to tremble in the depths of my soul. But I was so accustomed to separating reality into different planes and categories of thought that I soon found myself lost in this spectacle, still new and strange to my tyro mind, of a cosmos in which the dimensions of divine reality, of spirit, and of matter were also intimately mingled.[138]

In a similar, recent example, Catherine Vincie applies this extension of the real presence of the Eucharist to our expanding knowledge in the areas of ecological and evolutionary biology and cosmological physics that serve as the foundation of the Epic of Evolution as well as to our contemporary pluralistic context in which Christian sacramental life exists: "We must expand our imaginations to include in the communion of Christ those of other faith traditions and those who are not believers, as well as the community of Earth and the billions of galaxies that fill our skies. Christ is the Alpha of the universe; he is the new beginning, not the end."[139] Vincie's placement of this conversation within the increasingly pluralistic cultures in which Christianity is practiced in many parts of the world is important. What I have dealt with to this point in this chapter has been largely an insider conversation, and there is nothing wrong with this since the Eucharist, for Christians, is the primary ritual act through which we gain access to a broader ecological and cosmic sense of sacramentality. However, we must be cognizant of and humble enough to admit that Christian worship does not provide the exclusive means to access this sacramentality. As Sallie McFague points out, an ecological Christology should avoid falling into "Jesusolatry" by recognizing that "Jesus is the finger pointing to the moon."[140]

I would like to suggest that the Christian community can resist such exclusivist temptations when applying the Eucharist to an understanding that we live in a sacramental universe by recognizing that the presence of God that is revealed in a unique way in the life of Jesus is the same God who is still present with us, Christian and non-Christian, religious and non-religious. Stated in a slightly different way, the divine source of the universe and the life that has emerged and is still emerging from it is the same source of grace that was present in the life of Jesus. This sacramental grace can be experienced and embraced regardless of one's religious affiliation, and, I would argue even further, regardless of whether one is a theist or non-theist.[141] As Christians, we can acknowledge and accept the potential validity of other worldviews while maintaining the commitment that we are oriented to this presence sacramentally through our association with the bodily incarnation of God in Jesus. The historical centrality in Christian tradition of the life and revelation of God in Jesus connects Christian worshippers through Eucharistic practice to a potential encounter with the real presence of the divine in all things, a presence that binds everything that exists together in a vast interconnected divine embrace. There is an aspect of anamnesis, of remembering, connected with this understanding of the bodily presence of Christ in the Eucharist, but such a perspective, in the words of Lizette Larson-Miller, is "not a simple remembering of a past event but an acknowledgment of all that God has done and a recognition of the present reality of all God's actions and mercy."[142] In brief, the presence of the one who was incarnate in Jesus is present to us in the material substances that we receive in the liturgy of the Eucharist, and we should receive that grace with thanksgiving, which is, in fact, the meaning of the term Eucharist.

If we take such an understanding of the incarnation and its implications for a sacramental universe filled with ecological grace seriously, then everything is capable of having sacramental value.[143] From a Christian perspective, this is not in addition to but as a result of our understanding that God became incarnate in the person of Jesus Christ. In his description of the host that expanded to include all of creation, Teilhard de Chardin adds that "in actual fact the immense host, having given life to everything and purified everything, *was now slowly contracting*; and the treasures it was drawing into itself were joyously pressed together within its living light."[144] I think that Teilhard de Chardin's mystical vision is illustrative of how the sacramental worship of the Eucharist relates to the expanded sacramentality of a sacramental universe. Our experience of the real presence in the substances of the bread and wine received in the Eucharist expands our awareness of God's grace in all of the natural world. Yet, the Eucharist does not have an outward trajectory alone as it continuously draws us back in as a community of the faithful to glorify the gifts of creation in worship and to experience the mysterious presence of Christ so that we can be returned again and again into the wider world with the reminder that God is Emmanuel, "God with us," in order to emulate the self-giving sacrifice of Jesus in the lives we lead in our cultural and ecological communities.

V. Conclusion

Of course, there will be other interpretations of the Eucharist that continue to exist in Christian theological discourse, some of them more compatible with the scientific view of the Epic of Evolution and others less so. However, I would argue that a Eucharistic theology of ecological grace is an appropriate and credible expression of Christian tradition. It maintains the perspective that the Eucharist serves as our primary orientation to sacramental grace without on the one hand distorting the tradition in order to cohere with the narrative of the Epic of Evolution or, on the other, allowing the tradition to distort a proper understanding of the ecological and evolutionary process of life from which we emerged and upon which we depend for our continued sustenance. Furthermore, a proper understanding of the tradition of Eucharistic practice makes it clear that the trajectory of the Eucharist is such that it can reach out to heal not only human communities but also to alleviate the degradation of all life on Earth.

It is my opinion that the very heart of Christian faith, worship, and theology is predicated on Jesus' claim in the Synoptic gospels that the greatest commandments are loving God and loving one's neighbor as oneself.[145] If one interprets these commandments sacramentally, then they are best understood not as separate commandments but instead should be interpreted as the second fulfilling the first. In other words, we love God by loving life which only exists for us in embodiment. Furthermore, the emphasis of Jesus' life and teaching as it has been passed down to us in tradition makes it clear that what constitutes our neighbor should be characterized by an ever-widening circle. Bradshaw and Johnson cite Jesus' "apparent disregard for some of the established customs of the pious society of his day with regard to meals." By doing this, they claim, Jesus was clearly "moving the boundary markers with regard to those whom his contemporaries deemed acceptable to God and challenging the conventional divisions within society."[146] It is not difficult to imagine that circle widening further to include, in the words of American environmentalist Aldo Leopold, "the integrity, stability, and beauty of the biotic community."[147] Therefore, the implications for loving God through love of neighbor in this manner are that all of life becomes a form of sacramental worship.

This greatest of all commandments intimately links us with the life of Jesus in being responsible, as humans, for offering our own self-giving sacrifice in the lives we lead for the fulfillment of the potential of God's ever-present grace in the evolving divine creation. Furthermore, our experience of the incarnation and the self-giving sacrifice of Jesus embodied in the Eucharist can be lived out in Christian life by following Jesus' "way" of selfless love for God through love of neighbor. Morrill grounds the Eucharistic liturgy in the story of the road to Emmaus from the Gospel of Luke where the disciples only become aware of the identity of the risen Jesus following the breaking of bread in a ritual meal.[148] He describes the significance of this foundational story as follows: "In light of the sacramental action, the full force of the word the Lord had proclaimed in their company sets their hearts blazing and their feet back on the road. Only now, however, they hit the road with purpose, the mission of bringing the message of Christ crucified to life for the world."[149] This experience is available to us as well each time we approach the Eucharistic table to acknowledge the beautiful mystery that a real divine presence infuses all of life and that life continues to emerge from death as the evolutionary epic continues on, perpetuating ecological value through the loving grace of God in a sacramental universe. Embracing such a Eucharistic theology of ecological grace allows us to give thanks for this gift of life by glorifying God through the preservation of the evolving sacramental ecology from which all life emerges.

Chapter Four

Toward a Sacramental Ecology: The Role of the Priesthood in a Sacramental Universe

I. Introduction

If the sacramental tradition of the Eucharist is to successfully connect the Christian community with the ecological meaning and significance associated with the Epic of Evolution, it will be the role of the church's priesthood to lead the way. Therefore, the purpose of this chapter is to examine the sacramental role of the priesthood for developing an effective expression of Christian protection of the natural environment. I will argue that, in the role of administering the sacraments, priests have the responsibility not only of cultivating an understanding of the presence of Divine grace in the material substances of oil, bread, wine, and water, but also of projecting this awareness beyond the walls of the church and the ritual practice of individual sacraments to include all of God's creative order.

One of the tensions associated with a religious understanding of the Epic of Evolution is how it relates to and whether it can be effectively correlated with existing religious practice. Because the sacramental tradition of the church provides the opportunity of seamlessly relating the ecological value that emerges from the Epic of Evolution with the understanding of the conveyance of grace in Christian worship, I will argue that the priesthood potentially serves a significant role in connecting Christian worship to the larger ecological and evolutionary context in which it exists. Furthermore, through sacramental worship, this responsibility can be extended to include the concept of the priesthood of all believers so that all Christians, clergy and laity, can potentially serve the role of priests of Creation. In brief, as a means of promoting the human recognition of and orientation toward the manifestations of Divine grace in our necessarily ecological and evolutionary context, the practice of the priesthood is integral to the perpetuation of an effective Christian practice of caring for all of God's good Earth.

II. The Priesthood in an Ecological Context

The priesthood and sacramental tradition can never truly be spoken of in separation as the priestly role is inextricably bound with the administration of the sacraments, whether in a liturgically formal sense of the prescribed sacraments of the church or through a recognition of the presence of God's grace in all aspects of the created order. As a result, any discussion of the role of the human priesthood of God's continuing Creation must be understood to be inextricably bound to a sacramental, as well as ecological context. In the words of Elizabeth Theokritoff, the language of priesthood "cannot be understood apart from the idea of a cosmic liturgy in which all creatures play their part."[150]

Therefore, it is the role of the human priest to serve as a guide for the realization of divine grace in the formal sacraments of the Church as well as in the source and sustenance of all of our lives which is provided through Divine creativity. A report from the Mission and Public Affairs Council of the Church of England states the following: "By developing and using the earthly gifts of God rightly, human beings accept and help them realize their potential as communicators of God's reality. This is a microcosm of the priestly role in relation to the earth as a whole. Human beings should transform nature with the understanding that it is a gift of God, knowing that once the transformation is effected, the creation must be offered back to God."[151] Of course, we must be careful with how we use the term "transform"; however, in an ecological context, it must be accepted that human existence is necessarily characterized by a transformation of the environments in which we live. The question is how this transformation takes place and whether it is beneficial for the creation which is being transformed. By viewing the natural world sacramentally and therefore as a source of divine grace, the model of the priesthood, as the "mediator" or, perhaps more appropriately, the one who cultivates recognition of the grace that is present in all aspects of creation, can be understood as an appropriate contribution to the cultivation of sustainable human communities.

Furthermore, through an understanding of a cosmic liturgy, the priesthood becomes the primary means through which the church cultivates a proper and therefore mutually beneficial relationship with the rest of creation. According to the Church of England's statement *Sharing God's Planet*, in the Eucharist, the "elements of earthly reality, the bread and wine, become a means of grace for human beings and also themselves receive new meaning and status as they are offered to God."[152] However, the role of the priesthood extends beyond this as the grace present in the Eucharist is understood to be realizable in all aspects of material reality. Therefore, "human beings have the choice to live sacramentally, receiving all creation as a gift, transforming it and returning it to God, or to live selfishly, separating creation from its source and accruing it to themselves exclusively."[153]

Herein lies the significance of the priesthood and, concurrently, the sacramental life of the Church for the development of a symbiotic relationship between Christian communities and the ecological communities of which they are inextricably a part. The Eucharist, the primary sacrament of the Church, is inextricably bound with an extension of the formal liturgy into a cosmic liturgy, which offers the potential to sacralize the entire cosmos. In brief, it is the role of the ordained priest to provide the means through which the divine is conveyed through the bread and wine of the Eucharist and the role of the human priesthood in general to extend this sacramental understanding in order to cultivate an understanding of the presence of sacramental grace in all of the creative, natural order. In the words of John Habgood, "The priestly role of all human beings toward the world of nature entails a[n] ... offering through prayer and through the recognition that all belongs to God already, a similar transformation by the release of new potential and by the discovery that even in the world of nature there can be glimpses of heaven and earth."[154]

However, though priesthood language provides a way for us to understand the natural world sacramentally, there are aspects in the thought of some theologians who have written on the concept of the priesthood of creation that have led to criticisms of anthropocentrism due to the dependence of a human priesthood in offering creation to God. For instance, Theokritoff claims that one of the central themes of the priesthood model is "the key and indispensable role of the human being in bringing God's purposes for creation to their ultimate fulfillment."[155] Furthermore, consider the following statement from John Zizioulas on the idea of the "priest of creation":

Because man, unlike the angels ... forms an organic part of the material world, being the highest point in its evolution, he is able to carry with him the whole of creation to its transcendence. The fact that the human being is also an *animal*, far from being an insult to the human race, constitutes the *sine qua non* for his glorious mission in creation. If man gave up his claim to absolute freedom, the whole creation would automatically lose its hope for survival.[156]

What is active here is an understanding of the human priesthood as necessary for the rest of the creation, which, at least implicitly, certainly implies an anthropocentric aspect of the notion of the priesthood of creation.

Such anthropocentric understandings of the priesthood are unfortunately not isolated. For instance, Paulos Gregorios holds that humankind is a mediator in the strictest understanding of the term as a bridge between God and the rest of God's creation. For Gregorios, this mediating position is achieved through the incarnation of Jesus Christ which has reconciled humanity to God, and consequently God to humanity:

> Man is a mediator. He is poised between two realities—God and the world. He shares in both, he is united to both. He cannot live apart from either. That is the meaning of the incarnation of Jesus Christ. The only humanity that can survive is the new humanity, the humanity that has now been inseparably, indivisibly united with God in Jesus Christ. And because of its locus in the one divine-human nature of Christ, the new humanity is a mediating humanity—a humanity that reconciles and unites God and the world. It is an incarnate humanity—a humanity that is an inseparable part of the whole creation and inseparably united to the creator.[157]

In other words, according to Gregorios, humankind is a necessary link of reconciliation between the created order and God, which implies that there is no direct relation or manifestation of divine grace outside of the mediation of the human priesthood. Philip Sherrard offers a similar sentiment when he claims that "it is only through man fulfilling his role as mediator between God and the world that the world itself can fulfill its destiny and be transfigured in the light and presence of God It is in this sense that man ... is also and above all a priest—the priest of God: he who offers the world to God in his praise and worship and who simultaneously bestows divine love and beauty upon the world."[158] The problem arises not necessarily with the understanding of the priest as mediator but with the insistence that this mediation is exclusively maintained in a human priesthood separate from the rest of divine creation. There is no problem with making a distinction between humanity and non-human creation; however, there is a problem with interpreting this in a manner which claims that humanity is the sole medium through which non-human nature can commune with and, in some sense, worship God.

Much of the difficult language present here is bound up with a Christian understanding of the Fall and the doctrine of Original Sin. I do not want to go into a discussion of this here any further than to state that any understanding of the Fall in relation to a sacramental ecology should be seen as the human propensity for sin and not as an indelible mark suffered by humanity and non-human creation alike as a result of a mythical, primordial sin. More of a concern for the potential effectiveness of the priesthood model to seamlessly connect with the evolutionary epic is that theologians such as Gregorios and Sherrard mistakenly place theology in competition with science. For example, Sherrard, in particular, explicitly castigates modern science as the cause of "an ever-accelerating dehumanization of man and of the forms of his society, with all of the repercussions that this has had, and is still having, in the realm of nature."[159] While critiques of the desacralization of the natural environment by scientific worldviews are certainly not unfounded, a separation of theology from an understanding of an evolutionary and ecological framework is ultimately damaging to a theological approach to the natural environment and, consequently, to a proper Christian approach to ecological conservation.

Citing both Gregorios and Sherrard, Michael Northcott picks up on this in his criticism of the priesthood model. Referencing Sherrard's understanding of the role of the priesthood, Northcott claims that "it is doubtful that his humanocentric concept of humanity's priesthood in relation to created order, and his total rejection of the value of empirical observation of the world as a means to understanding this order, is productive of an environmental ethic which allows nature apart from human purposes the space to *be*."[160] He goes on to emphasize that, in his opinion, "the concept of humanity's priestly role in relation to creation is deeply humanocentric and seems to encourage the remaking and hominisation of the whole biosphere in the human image and for the needs of the human body. Nature or creation by this metaphor is denied any independent or intrinsic value."[161]

Despite the problems presented by the way in which the language of the priesthood of creation has been used by some theologians for the purpose of addressing ecological concerns, the priesthood model need not be presented in a manner that implies the exclusive access of the human priest to the divine as a mediator for the rest of creation. Theokritoff defends the priesthood model against criticisms such as Northcott's by claiming that the priesthood model is, in fact, not anthropocentric but theocentric. She offers an understanding of the priesthood model "predicated on the assumption that while every creature has some *direct* relationship with God, no creature has an *exclusive* relationship with God such that the quality of the rest of creation's relationship is of no importance to it."[162] Further, she states that "there is a growing tendency to emphasize the active role of other creatures: they are not only the substance of the offering, but also concelebrants in the offering of glory to God.... And it is precisely God's relationship with all creation that necessitates our 'priestly' engagement with the rest of creation, not to serve our own purposes but to serve his."[163] As a result, the human role as priest of creation is necessary in her view but does not preclude the opportunity for divine grace to be mediated through other aspects of creation in addition to the role of the human priesthood in offering an awareness of and orientation to the divine grace that is present to all in the creation which is provided through God's loving creativity. Still, what then does this say about the significance of the perceived necessity of a human priesthood, in relation to non-human creation, as a means of sacramentally expressing this divine grace and offering it as a form of worship to God?

According to Theokritoff, the "real stumbling block presented by the notion of human priesthood ... seems to be not the idea that the human manner of offering is in some way unique, but the implication that the offering of other creatures requires some fulfillment that humans alone can provide."[164] It seems to me that it is not necessary for a human priesthood to glorify the rest of nature. This type of understanding would conflict with a scientific understanding of the evolutionary process and the acceptance of the contingency of the human species as we currently exist. Instead, the priesthood of creation is an example of a particular mode of human worship of the Creator. However, in a necessarily interconnected ecological context, perhaps Theokritoff is correct in claiming that while nature "can and does image God's glory by itself; the offering of creation as a whole is incomplete unless humans turn their awareness of the world around them into their own offering of thanksgiving."[165] In other words, given the human influence on our planet, if we fail to live out the human priesthood and therefore view the world sacramentally, then we are a detriment to the expression of divine grace that can be realized through the creation.

Therefore, the priest need not be understood as a mediator, in the exclusive sense of serving as a necessary means through which grace is channeled to the rest of the worldly creation but instead can be envisioned as someone whose function is to cultivate the awareness of the grace of God in all things. Sometimes this is more explicit in terms of being in the form of the bread and wine in the Eucharist, but a specific sacramental "celebration" or "thanksgiving" can be extended to include all aspects of the created order. Furthermore, the rest of creation doesn't need a human priesthood, but we properly include the rest of creation in our particular, unique expression of worship of the source of the entirety of creation. Perhaps, in this way, we are fulfilling the Imago Dei by recognizing and valuing the goodness of all aspects of creation as they point toward the Divine wellspring of life.

III. Ecological Grace and the Sacramental Role of the Priesthood

In this section, I would like to further examine the importance of the sacrament of the Eucharist for developing an ecologically credible form of Christian worship. In the two preceding chapters, I explained how the Eucharist will be able to extend beyond an understanding of communion as a singular event which happens within the church to an understanding of the sacramental significance for all of creation. The potential significance of such an extension is clear. In the words of Ian Barbour, "Even greater value is attributed to nature when it is believed that the sacred is present in and under it."[166] Fortunately, this is not difficult to do in the sense that, instead of being seen as an isolated event, the Eucharist, properly understood, should be understood as an event that carries with it significance for the entire creation in that it serves as a representation of the sacramentality of all aspects of God's creation.

According to Arthur Peacocke, if "we as individuals and as communities so will, we can indeed be co-creating creatures of and with God in the work of integrating the human-made and God-made constituents of the world—that is, in 'making it whole,' which is what, in its root meaning, 'salvation' means."[167] This is an interesting comment on the relationship between the human, built environment and the natural environment, the human relationship to the God given creation of which we are inextricably a part. Interestingly, Peacocke envisions this relationship in terms of the sacraments with the Eucharist representing, in microcosm, the human co-creation with God in terms of the liturgical realization of divine grace through the sacraments: "Because it is bread and not corn, wine and not grapes, that are consecrated, this act has come to be experienced also as a new evaluation of the work of *humanity* in *co-creating with God in ordinary work.*"[168] Therefore, our creativity, in some sense, participates with the creative action of God in the Eucharist. In this way, we can begin to learn how to relate human action with divine action to the mutual benefit of human culture and non-human creation.

It is necessary to clarify that this co-creation is not understood as a co-creation of divine grace. Instead, as Peacocke points out, "God is already at work 'in, with and under' the natural processes of the world ... God's grace is already operative in the world."[169] Therefore, the "proper responses of human beings to nature at once suggests that their role may be conceived as that of *priests of creation*, indeed as *ministers of grace*, as a result of whose activity the sacrament of nature is reverenced."[170] In other words, through the ordained priesthood's role of administering the sacraments and through the human priesthood of creation in general, we participate in the production of that through which divine grace is understood to be imparted.

Avoiding the language of co-creation, John Habgood presents an understanding of the Eucharist as the sacramental act through which we recognize and react to the grace present in creation at large. In his words: "The eucharist is a complex act of giving and receiving in which the worshipers as well as God are both givers and receivers. At its highest it is a mutual exchange of love. But all this is set within the context of what God has already done. Despite the mutuality, therefore, the keyword is *response*. Sacramental action is thus essentially a matter of cooperation rather than co-creation. As human beings we share a role with God in drawing out the divine potential of the world, but only because God has already ... taken the decisive steps."[171] As I will discuss below, I think that Habgood's language of response to the divine action that is present in creation is a very effective means of conveying the significant role of the human priesthood in conveying the value in the created order that must necessarily be recognized if we are to value the ecological connectedness from which all life emerges.

While Theokritoff is clear that the role of the human priesthood is not to manipulate nature, she offers an understanding of the Eucharist with a heavy emphasis on transformation as opposed to response or co-creation.[172] In her words: "The Eucharist is not simply an offering of praise and thanks, as other church services are, but an offering of thanks that *meets with a divine response* whereby the created offering is transformed. To speak of a cosmic eucharist, then, is to say that creation's praise, however adequate as an offering, is not in itself perfect: it too needs to be transformed."[173]

Integral to each of these sacramental understandings is the notion of the human priesthood cultivating the human recognition of and response to the Eucharist and nature as it is given to us on this earth as sacrament. However, I think that we need to be careful with the language of transformation in the sense that the medium (i.e., material creation) through which divine grace is conveyed is inferior. Of course, this language draws upon the idea of the Fall and Original Sin. Theokritoff clearly has this in mind when she writes the following: "Whether the fall of the human creature literally introduced death and decay into the world or signaled failure to transcend an existing state of death and decay, the conclusion remains that material creation is not now in its intended state, and that we bear a responsibility for this."[174] If this statement is interpreted in terms of the harm humans as a species have done to the ecological communities of which we are a part, then it is effective. However, Christians can have an eschatological hope of a new heaven and new earth without treating our current setting as if it is innately deficient. Therefore, sacramental transformation is more effective if it is understood as recognition of the grace present in the created order, which points to the need to restore that which has been degraded in creation, than as a necessary change to that which is in need of improvement because of an inherent deficiency.

In summary, the transformation which takes place in the Eucharist is the work of God and not the work of humans; therefore, the grace that comes through the sacrament of nature is not characterized by priestly manipulation of nature but as a recognition and appreciation for the grace within all of the created order. In other words, the "transformation" is not a singular act enacted by the human priest. Instead, the role of the priest is to point toward and orient the community of the church to the presence of divine grace in the elements of the bread and wine, which also serve as a representative example of the divine grace present within all of creation. Habgood expresses this sentiment very clearly: "Church and sacraments are the making visible of what is already there but might otherwise remain unrecognized."[175] Furthermore, he writes: "The essential point is that material reality is shown to be capable of bearing the image of the divine.... Thus what happens to water, bread, and wine when used as vehicles of God's grace is no isolated miracle. All matter shares this potential, and specific sacramental actions ... are the God-given means by which this truth is safeguarded and made known."[176] Therefore, the grace bestowed through the Eucharist is not unique to this particular sacrament but an icon for the sacramental potential of the blessing of life as it is given to us in all aspects of life on this planet. The importance of recognizing such an understanding through the sacramental offering of the Eucharist cannot be overstated.

IV. Problems and Possibilities for an Ecological Priesthood

It seems clear to me that the model of the priesthood of creation provides a very effective and ecologically credible framework for Christian traditions which are oriented around a traditional sacramental approach to worship with the priestly office providing leadership and guidance for the realization of the divine grace that is present to all in our sacramental universe. However, such a model can potentially cause tension in other Christian communities. For instance, Theokritoff claims that when "people take exception to the idea of man being 'priest of creation,' it seems to be because to them, 'priesthood' implies clericalism—an exclusive class of people who control everyone else's access to God."[177] This example points to potential limitations that such a model may present given the residual baggage of priesthood terminology in many post-Reformation contexts; however, I would like to suggest that these misunderstandings and preconceived notions can be avoided so that this model can be more widely applied in Christian communities attempting to establish effective environmental ministries.

In fact, even among those Christian traditions that have been most susceptible to stigmatizing the terminology of priesthood, the priesthood model can be incorporated by an appeal to the Protestant notion of the "priesthood of all believers." Furthermore, while the liturgical and sacramental life of Christian churches may be stressed more heavily in some traditions than in others, the primary sacrament of the Eucharist as a thanksgiving and re-creation of the Gospel version of the Last Supper of Jesus carries significance in all forms of Christian worship. Laura Yordy expresses this as follows: "Regardless of a church's particular Eucharistic theology, the elements of bread and wine are the most significant material expression of Christian worship."[178] Whether practiced daily, weekly, or relatively infrequently, the Eucharist is the primary sacrament of the Christian Church and, with Baptism, one of two sacraments that are universally recognized by Christian communities. Consequently, the sacramental aspect of the priesthood model can potentially be a point of agreement between all Christians instead of a barrier to the use of certain language in particular Christian communities.

Therefore, the priesthood in relation to sacramental life and therefore the divine grace present in creation need not be understood in terms of a perceived clericalism characterized by claims of exclusive access to God on the part of a select few. According to Habgood, "The sacraments entail human cooperation with divine initiative, a cooperation which is essentially priestly. This is so whether we think in terms of the priesthood of all believers or the representative priesthood of individuals within the body of the church."[179] In other words, the priestly role of humanity includes but extends beyond the formal, ordained priesthood in a manner that allows clergy and lay people alike to participate and, in some sense, aid in perpetuating the grace of creation.

Echoing a similar sentiment, Theokritoff claims that the priesthood model offers an understanding of the human, and specifically Christian, relationship with the natural environment, which is lacking in the stewardship model, the model, which is perhaps the most prevalent of all the models of Christian response to environmental conservation and certainly the most popular among Protestant Christians, those who are most likely to have a problem with the priestly approach. She writes: "The language of human 'priesthood' in creation ... serves as a useful counterbalance to the Protestant language of 'stewardship' which has gained wide currency even in secular circles, but which ties us too closely to notions of property and economics. The language of 'priesthood' underlines the Godwardness of creation as a whole: it leads us to see our habitat as an 'immense cathedral' and our daily life as a Eucharist."[180] This is not meant to imply that the stewardship model cannot still be useful; instead, what these examples exhibit is that the model of the priesthood of creation need not be understood as applicable only to those

Christian communities that emphasize a liturgical orientation for worship and the priesthood as the office through which the sacraments are administered. Alternately, the priesthood model can be effectively applied to any Christian community attempting to cultivate a Christian connection with the natural environment that is true to the necessarily sacramental nature of the Church and simultaneously ecologically credible.

In the full expression of the priestly model, this begins, in Christian worship, with those who administer the sacraments but emanates outward to include all of creation as a source through which to receive sacramental grace. According to Northcott, the "enormous value of a sacramental approach ... is that it makes every Sunday eucharist a powerful ecological parable of the capacity of matter itself to be redolent of the redemptive purposes of God for the creation and to mediate God's grace to the Eucharistic participants. The transformation of bread and wine into elements which mediate the presence of Christ is a reiteration of the potential of all material existence to reveal God's grace."[181] In a similar example, Theokritoff offers an apt metaphor for the relationship between the priest and congregation and humanity and non-human creation: "Just as the ordained priesthood has the task of fulfilling the offering of the whole people of God, so humanity as the 'priesthood of creation' should be seen not as displacing the offering of all created things, but as affirming and furthering that offering."[182] Therefore, the priesthood can only effectively convey the presence of divine grace in a communal setting whether this be in participation with members of the church or as members of the human species participating in the life drama of the ongoing divine creation on our planet. The result is that the priesthood model is highly adaptable as long as the church community that is seeking to incorporate it is willing to accept the corporate and therefore interconnected character of sacramental worship in the presence of the divine grace exhibited through God's creation.

V. Priesthood and the Sacramental Community of the Church

The emphasis on the ecclesiastical community binds us not only to our fellow members of the Church but also to the entire creation, human and non-human alike. Therefore, the sacramental and liturgical emphasis on community promotes an ecological understanding of connectedness which can be applied, through a sacramental understanding of our world, to all of creation. Referring to the language of the "priesthood of creation" Theokritoff writes:

> It is no coincidence that this language came to prominence against the backdrop of a profound rediscovery of the Church as a *body* in which all members, and all orders, have a vital role to play. It is a body characterized by *sobernost*—unity in diversity, communion and interdependence. We should immediately recognize the similarity between this vision of how the Church community functions, and our growing understanding of how the earth community functions.[183]

As implied previously, the priestly role in promoting the community of participants as fellow priests of creation is further emphasized in the Eucharist. In Habgood's words, "The theme of cooperation receives further emphasis in the communion, which forms the climax of the whole. There can be no true giving and receiving with God unless others form a part of it.... The microcosm of love and mutuality in response to the love of God experienced by those engaged in sacramental worship ultimately has to include the macrocosm."[184] Therefore, the priestly role is understood, in this sense, as a binding together of members of the community of believers in order to experience the grace of sacramental worship in the material substance of the Eucharist as well as in the cultivation, through a proper understanding of the Eucharist, of the awareness of the sacramental nature of the creation itself as it is revealed to us in our daily lives.

VI. Conclusion

What I have attempted to convey in this chapter is that the model of the priesthood is not only a viable but an integral aspect of Christian environmental ministries. In addition, I have claimed that the priest's role of administering the sacraments, in particular the Eucharist, which is the primary sacramental orientation for Christian communities, provides an example for the way in which Christian communities can become the priests of all of creation. My argument is that this is an issue not of any exclusive rite but of revealing or cultivating the awareness of the divine grace in the presence of the bread and wine of the Eucharistic meal as well as, in extension, the entire creation of which humans are only a part. Therefore, the priesthood is our unique opportunity to offer worship for the source of all creation through an understanding and orientation toward the grace realized through a sacramental approach to all aspects of the divine natural, creative order.

Receiving Christ, through whom, according to Scripture, all things came into being, in the Eucharist forms an intimate link between the formal sacramental life of the church and the understanding of the sacrament of all creation, between the ordained priesthood and the human priesthood in general. The latter of which consists of all members of the ecclesiastical community who are called to cultivate an awareness and respect for the grace present within the life that has emerged from the evolutionary and ecological development of planet Earth. Therefore, the Eucharist and creation are intimately linked in the life of the church. The Eucharist, as the primary sacrament and orienting liturgical act of the church community, is the means through which the members of the community are instructed by the teachings of the church and the ordained priesthood to become priests of creation through the recognition, awareness, and subsequent response to the sacramental nature of the entirety of creation. Therefore, the priesthood and, consequently, the Eucharistic sacrament truly has cosmic significance and provides an effective means through which a valuation for and protection of the evolving divine creation can be achieved through the sacramental life of the Christian community.

Chapter Five

A Grandeur in this View of Life: The Ecological Significance of Tradition and Sacrament in the Theology of David Brown

I. Introduction

The title of this chapter is taken from the final lines of Charles Darwin's *On the Origin of Species* where he wrote, in reference to his theory of evolution by natural selection, that there "is grandeur in this view of life, with its several powers, having been originally breathed into a few forms or into one; and that whilst this planet has gone cycling on according to the fixed law of gravity, from so simple a beginning endless forms most beautiful and most wonderful have been, and are being, evolved."[185] The following will serve as the final chapter of this book in which I have examined the ecological and religious significance of the narrative of this natural history of life on Earth, commonly referred to as the Epic of Evolution.[186] In brief, I contend that the attribution of value that emerges from an understanding of the evolutionary and ecological connectedness of the Epic of Evolution can seamlessly correlate with the sacramental tradition of the Christian Church to the mutual enhancement of ecological conservation efforts and Christian sacramental worship. In the preceding chapters, I argued that the Christian sacraments, with a particular emphasis on the Eucharist, are a part of a larger sacramentality an understanding of which allows for the potential experience of God's grace in all of material reality.[187]

In Chapter Four, I assessed the sacramental role of the Church's priesthood in fostering a connection between Eucharistic sacramental worship in Christian tradition and a broader sense of sacramentality that coheres with the Epic of

Evolution in assigning value to the ecological connectedness that is the source and sustenance of all life on Earth. If such an attempt is to be uniquely Christian in identity as well as relevant to the issue of modern ecological concern it is intended to address, it is necessary that the theological argument offered be simultaneously consistent with a theological perspective emerging from Christian tradition and credible to the contemporary context in which it is applied.[188] In this final chapter, I will argue that David Brown's sacramental theology offers a model theological framework for accomplishing the correlation between ecological value and sacramental grace with a particular emphasis, toward the end of the chapter, on the Eucharist. In brief, I will maintain that Brown's understanding of the concepts of sacrament and tradition can be used as a means to strengthen and expand the sacramental significance of Christian worship in a way that is relevant not only for Christian tradition but also for an understanding and appreciation of and value for our necessarily evolutionary and ecological context.

II. Sacrament, Sacramentality, and the Re-enchantment of Nature

In *God and Enchantment of Place: Reclaiming Human Experience*, Brown advocates for an expansion of our understanding of the sacraments as a means to achieve a broader sense of sacramentality in order to increase potential sites of contemporary religious experience.[189] Before the sacraments were formally outlined at seven by Peter Lombard in the twelfth century and later fixed at that number at the Council of Lyons in the thirteenth, he claims that such a broadened sacramentality was quite common during the first millennium of Christian history.[190] Referring to this earlier understanding of sacrament, he writes: "The word eventually came to be used to cover a far wider range of significance than the traditional sacraments might ever have led us to expect.... In effect 'sacrament' had come to mean any mysterious indwelling that anticipates or points to some greater reality."[191] Understood in this way, religious experience can be lived out in a "sacramental universe" where life is considered as "coming as a generous, divine gift."[192] Consequently, sacramental grace is not confined to the formal sacraments of the Church but permeates God's ongoing Creation if we will only take the time to make ourselves aware of it.

For Brown, to once again embed the sacraments of the Church within a larger sense of sacramentality will serve not only as a renewal of religious experience but also encourage the Church toward a more appropriate understanding of God's relationship with all of the created order. Such a move is both necessary and appropriate, he contends, because the retreat from a broader understanding of sacramentality has resulted in limiting the range and significance of the worship life of the Church and, consequently, the Church's influence on the wider culture in which it exists. For example, as a result of the sacraments being treated far too frequently as "quintessentially 'churchy'," the Church's sacramental worship has been pushed to the margins of the wider world in which we live our lives. Brown describes this development as follows: "Whereas it was once inconceivable for human beings to think religion irrelevant to their lives, now more often than not it functions (at least in the developed world) more like an optional extra, almost like just yet one more competing leisure activity."[193] To remedy this, Brown claims that a "God active outside the control of the Church needs to be acknowledged, and the implications heeded."[194] What is needed therefore is a renewal of the understanding of our experience of grace in the lives we live out in human cultures, which are part of the larger ecological communities of which we are all inextricably a part.[195]

Brown also relates this retreat of theological inquiry from a broader sacramentality to what Max Weber referred to as "the disenchantment of the world."[196] In brief, Weber implied that the rise of modern science fueled by the influence of Enlightenment thought led to the suppression of an understanding of mystery and value in the natural world when divine teleology was replaced with empirical explanations.[197] Brown argues for a re-enchantment of the world through a return to a view of the world "in which experience of the divine was once the norm and not the exception, and can be so again."[198] He argues that this can be achieved through his broadened vision of the sacraments grounded in what he refers to as "natural" or "implicit" religion. Referring to this natural religion, he writes: "Sport, drama, humour, dance, architecture, place and home, the natural world are all part of a long list of activities and forms of experience that have been relegated to the periphery of religious reflection, but which once made invaluable contributions to a human perception that this world is where God can be encountered, and encountered often."[199] In other words, re-enchantment is achieved through a sacramental expansion that potentially locates God's grace in all of material reality.

Such an extension of divine grace in all aspects of life is often distinguished in theological circles as general revelation in relation to the special revelation that is unique to the salvific role of the Church. However, Brown resists making such clear distinctions: "Crude contrasts between the 'specific' and the 'general' or 'universal' need therefore to be avoided. Potentially, all may function as experiences of God."[200] This may seem to diminish the role of the formal sacraments of the Church; however, this need not be the case. For example, the Eucharist will remain the primary form of ritual worship for Christian communities.[201] Yet, Brown's understanding of a broadened sacramentality does not allow for formal sacraments to be considered exclusive or insulating. He writes: "It is not that grace is something uniquely dispensed through the Christian community. God has been addressing humanity at large throughout human history both in its experience of the natural world and in the various ways in which it has expanded upon that experience in its own creativity."[202] Instead of being an isolated means of receiving divine grace, the formal sacraments function as part of an integrated whole pointing the worshiping community outward with an awareness that God's grace is potentially experienced in all aspects of our Earthly lives.

Brown is quick to point out that establishing criteria for such a view of the sacraments will not be easy and will be problematic for many.[203] Nevertheless, he is clear that a conservative theological criticism of such an approach will only hinder the significance of the Christian sacramental experience: "To acknowledge external factors does of course make criteria more difficult, but it seems to me that those who insist on purely internal ones are really engaging in a form of self-deception in supposing their own applications clear-cut."[204] In other words, to isolate the sacraments as exclusive conveyers of God's grace in separation or for protection from the larger world in which we exist not only ignores the realities of a potentially sacramental universe but diminishes the role of Christian sacraments in a world that is in desperate need of re-enchantment.

The ecological implications of Brown's sacramental theology are clear. By once again entering areas of divine presence that have been neglected by theologians for far too long, the sacramental life of the Church as well as the valuation for the ecological communities in which it exists can be strengthened. It is necessary to point out at this point that applying a Christian sacramental approach to the Epic of Evolution also implies a comment on tradition, a term that suggests a compatibility with development and change.[205] It is to the topic of Brown's understanding of tradition and how his sacramental approach relates to the larger Christian tradition from which it emerged as well as, potentially, to the ecological value associated with the evolutionary history of life that I now turn.

III. Tradition, Rooted and Emergent

Brown's sacramental theology can be more fully appreciated when read in the context of his work on tradition most notably developed in *Tradition and Imagination: Revelation and Change*, a book published in 1999 prior to *God and Enchantment of Place*. His sacramental theology is reflective of his understanding of tradition in that both are grounded in a broadening impetus that seeks to avoid isolating or limiting any aspect of Christian religious experience. Key to this understanding is a reassessment of the concepts of revelation and tradition where Christians are called to "disabuse themselves of the habit of contrasting biblical revelation and later tradition, and instead see the hand of God in a continuing process that encompasses both."[206] Furthermore, he contends that "the process of revelation had to continue beyond Scripture, since otherwise the tradition would have become stultified through being trapped within one particular epoch and its assumptions."[207] In essence, neither Scripture nor any era in post-biblical Christian tradition is distinguished as having a monopoly on or authoritative position in relation to the revelatory experience of God. That revelation is ever present sacramentally waiting to be recognized by and contribute to the ongoing tradition of the Church.

As his title implies, his interpretation of tradition is predicated heavily on the word "imagination," in his words, "not because I do not take doctrinal issues seriously, but because I regard them as secondary and parasitic on the stories and images that give religious belief its shape and vitality."[208] More conservative voices will certainly resist such a limitation of authority in relation to the primacy of the Scriptures as well as certain aspects of the tradition such as the theological doctrines that emerged from the early ecumenical councils. However, for Brown, this is not seen as a betrayal of the tradition but is instead an attempt to take seriously a living or "open" tradition that is perpetually informed by continuing divine revelation.[209] God's grace is ever present in material reality and should not be understood to be isolated within the life of the Church. Therefore, there is "the necessity for tradition to keep meanings alive not simply by preserving them but by allowing their constant adaptation as ... the trajectories from the past meet fresh triggers in new situations and thereby help generate new meanings."[210] Understood in this way, tradition maintains a rootedness in the development of past conceptions of Christian thought and practice while serving as the impetus to look forward to engage in new creative possibilities in the interpretation of divine revelation in the present.

This also involves a commitment to Christian tradition being potentially informed and transformed by the wider culture and ecological communities in which it exists. Brown writes:

> Though undoubtedly part of the strength of any particular tradition does lie in its internal structure and foundations, to give these the last word as well as the first would be to court disaster. A tradition flourishes not only through a healthy respect for its roots, but equally in lively confrontation with external pressures and influences whereby it is forced to think itself anew.[211]

Essentially, Brown's understanding of tradition allows the freedom to incorporate something in a contemporary context without it being understood as peripheral to the tradition it informs. As a result, potentially any aspect of life and culture can be embraced and applied without fear that it is extraneous. In doing so, Brown means "to challenge the common assumption that the power of revelation is necessarily undermined if external material from the surrounding culture is used to illuminate or even rewrite its story. That can happen, but need not if due care is taken to integrate what appeals to the pagan or secular imagination into an appropriate underlying Christian framework."[212] In brief, Christian history, of which Christian tradition is inextricably a part, is honored and valued, but the living tradition of the Church is not static and therefore, while always being informed by that history, must always remain open to being influenced by the contemporary context in which it exists.

Of course, accepting such a view of tradition is risky. By following Brown's view, one cannot withdraw from culture or retreat into a dogmatic interpretation of Scripture or Creedal formulation as an absolute authority. However, such a view, while potentially precarious, is the bravest step forward if we are going to simultaneously honor and ground our contemporary expressions in past tradition while achieving relevance and credibility as it is expressed in a wider cultural context. To quote Alfred North Whitehead: "That religion is strong which in its ritual and its modes of thought evokes an apprehension of the commanding vision. The worship of God is not a rule of safety— it is an adventure of the spirit, a flight after the unattainable. The death of religion comes with the repression of the high hope of adventure."[213] By boldly proclaiming the loving embrace and celebration of life within and beyond traditional boundaries, Brown's theological perspective pertaining to sacrament and tradition is in no danger of suffering such a death.

A Brief Case Study

In *Tradition and Imagination*, Brown finds potential influences for ongoing tradition in a range of places including visual art, non-Christian religions, and various cultural expressions of the Christmas story. I want to conclude this section with a brief discussion of the potential for Brown's theology to seamlessly connect sacramental grace with the ecological value associated with the evolutionary history of life on Earth by applying his understanding of sacramentality and open tradition to a couple of examples from religious environmentalism.

In an essay entitled "'A generous God': the sacramental vision of David Brown," Robert MacSwain cites American environmentalist Edward Abbey's criticism of Christianity as an "'indoor' religion" and claims that, in Abbey, Brown finds a "surprising ally."[214] However, according to MacSwain, "whereas Abbey thinks that Christianity is irredeemably and essentially an 'indoor' affair, Brown sees this as a relatively new and potentially redeemable state of affairs."[215] This criticism of Christian tradition as limited in relation to its potential to address issues of environmental concern is not an uncommon one in contemporary environmental thought. As a result, I want to briefly take a look at two authors who are representative of the field of Religion and Ecology in order to examine further how Brown's theology might be applied in order to address this criticism.

Bron Taylor and Thomas Berry both look to the evolutionary emergence of life on Earth as the primary source of religious inspiration, and they both also offer critiques of Christian tradition that are applicable to the aspects of Brown's theological perspective discussed here. In *Dark Green Religion: Nature Spirituality and the Planetary Future*, Taylor defines "dark green religion" as "religion that considers nature to be sacred, imbued with intrinsic value, and worthy of reverent care" and argues "that it would be much easier to develop sustainable societies if religions were firmly grounded in an evolutionary-ecological worldview."[216] Making a clear distinction between an evolutionary-ecological perspective and traditional religious conceptions, he is skeptical at best that traditional religions can contribute significantly to a "dark green" worldview, reserving especially harsh criticism for what he refers to as "Abrahamic traditions." He writes: "Religious thinkers since Darwin have gone through excruciating contortions in their efforts to graft such a worldview onto their faith traditions, which generally consider essential some sort of nonmaterial spiritual dimension and one or more divine beings inhabiting it. The result simply fails the laugh test for many if not most scientifically literate people."[217]

Berry, a Catholic priest and self-professed "geologian," understands the universe as a divine manifestation and, as a result, he holds that the narrative story of the approximately 14-billion-year history of our universe and the life that has emerged from it should be viewed as "our primary revelatory experience."[218] This narrative is clearly juxtaposed with what he sees as the ecological limitations of Christianity relying solely on the biblical scriptures as the source of revelation. He claims that the "biblical story, however valid, however unique in what it offers, no longer seems sufficient to address the issues before us."[219] For Berry, the best way to embrace our modern ecological existence is through an acceptance of the religious understanding of the scientific narrative of the emergent creativity in our universe:

> Our greatest difficulty stems from the inability of our religious traditions to accept our new way of telling the story of the universe, which derives from our empirically driven data.... The effort to interpret our immediate experience of the universe simply through our scriptural data involves a serious distortion in our way of thinking. It subverts the very basis of our primordial experience of the divine in the manifestations offered us through the universal order of existence.[220]

If one takes Brown's theological perspective concerning sacrament and tradition seriously, one can engage with and counter such critical dismissals of the ecological significance of theistic tradition offered by Taylor as well as join with Berry in accepting the presence of the divine in all of material reality.

Berry calls on the role of the integral ecologist as a normative guide for our time to engage the "great spiritual mission of the present ... to renew all the traditional religious-spiritual traditions in the context of the integral functioning of the biosystems of the planet."[221] Brown's theological framework provides an opportunity for those who represent Christian tradition to fulfill such a role and avoid the criticism of Christianity being an isolated or "indoor" religion in practice. However, to be considered Christian, such a response must be recognizable as distinctly Christian in character. In the final section of this chapter, I will demonstrate the ways in which Brown's broadened sacramentality and open tradition are thoroughly grounded in the history of Christian thought and practice and therefore his understanding of the expansion of sacrament and tradition can be seen not as extraneous to but a strengthening of the tradition from which it emerged.

IV. Eucharist, Incarnation, and the Sacramental Grace of a "Generous God"

By presenting the sacraments as necessarily reaching beyond the borders of tradition to connect with and be influenced by larger cultural and ecological realities, Brown is making the assumption that such a framework can be consistent with a Christian identity. A criticism that will certainly arise is that his perspective stretches the traditional Christian understanding of sacrament and tradition beyond recognition. Therefore, it is necessary to explore further how this aspect of Brown's theology represents a uniquely Christian response to the issues of ecological value with which I am concerned here. With this in mind, I want to now turn attention toward the ways in which Brown's sacramental theology is thoroughly grounded in the formal sacrament of the Eucharist and demonstrate how this Eucharistic connection necessarily binds Christian tradition to a larger incarnational, sacramental reality.

In *God of Grace and Body: Sacrament in Ordinary*, Brown directly relates the sacramental presence of grace in all of God's ongoing Creation to the essential bodily nature of the Eucharist: "The activity of God is everywhere in the material world that is his creation, and not at all an isolated and occasional phenomena. That is why it seems to me no accident that Christianity's central sacrament focuses on body and on a human body at that. It is no mere 'spiritual' presence that is on offer in the eucharist but one envisaged in definitely material terms."[222] For Christians, the Eucharist is the primary sacramental rite carried out in a sacramental universe simultaneously sending the members of the gathered community out to connect with a broader sacramentality and drawing worshipers back in to this central ritual enactment ensuring that the Christian expression of sacramentality is unique to the tradition. Therefore, the recognition of the bodily presence in the Eucharist is both reflective of and provides a trajectory toward an awareness of God's grace in all of the evolving, created order. Accordingly, Brown asserts that "the eucharist is best viewed as the supreme sacrament not because it offers a complete contrast to the way the world is, but rather because it represents the culmination of how God is perceived to act elsewhere in the world, through material reality."[223]

The primacy of the Eucharist in relation to a broader sacramental reality also directly relates Brown's sacramental theology to a broadened understanding of the incarnation of a "generous God." In fact, he states that his justification for a tradition that is receptive to continuing revelation relies "heavily on assuming the truth of the incarnation."[224] For Brown, the incarnation of God in Jesus Christ "revealed a loving and merciful God who, while calling human beings back from sin, none the less fully endorsed our material world by himself becoming part of it."[225] However, like his understanding of sacrament and tradition, the incarnation is not an isolated event. If God is truly generous, he asks, "would we not expect to find him at work everywhere?"[226] Furthermore, if we fail to take the implications of a generous God seriously, he claims, "the less plausible does God's love of creation, and indeed his very existence, become."[227] For Brown, the generous God of the incarnation is "willing to focus his presence in a tiny wafer" yet is also available to be potentially recognized in all of the divine, natural order if we will only take the time to notice.[228] This recognition is made explicit in the Eucharist through the Eucharistic substances of bread and wine, whose form are the work of human hands. However, the grace present in these human products existed prior to their being offered in ritual thanksgiving, and as a result, in receiving communion, we are oriented to an incarnational sacramentality that extends well beyond the community gathered in formal liturgy to include the life sustaining ecological communities of Earth.

This suggests that, while Jesus will remain, for Christians, the definitive revelation for God in material reality, the incarnation of God is not a one-time event. In Brown's words, "for God to impact on every aspect of us immanence must also be claimed: God involved with matter. Christians believe that this happened at the deepest and most profound level in the incarnation, but if there is to be a continuing effect this cannot have happened just once, but must relate to all material existence."[229] From a Christian perspective, we can recognize this continuing divine activity through participation in the Eucharistic liturgy, which returns us time and again to the lives we lead in a necessarily ecological context with a broadened awareness of God's loving presence in all of the sacramental universe.[230] While some will bristle at what may seem an "unorthodox" approach, the intimate connection Brown's sacramental theology shares with divine incarnation and Eucharistic ritual practice makes his framework, I would argue, deeply and thoroughly embedded in the tradition.

V. Conclusion

Brown states that all divine communication "must be mediated in one way or another, given that God and human beings are so clearly two utterly different sorts of reality."[231] This mediation can take place through nature or culture, which includes the cultural creations of the Church and the wider culture beyond the Church's traditional boundaries as well as the entirety of the natural world.[232] Brown calls us to attend to all of these. It is, therefore, the role of the church to interpret how that mediation is to be expressed from the perspective of the Christian community. This will fall on anyone who speaks on behalf of Christian tradition but will particularly be the responsibility of the Church's priests who are called to administer the Church's sacraments.

Ultimately, all is predicated on the ecological. All material reality that is available to mediate the divine, including the traditions of the Church, has emerged from the evolutionary and cosmic history of Earthly life. Therefore, one can accurately say that the original sacramental substance, the evolving creation itself, can be understood through the cultivation of an awareness of the Epic of Evolution. This awareness, in turn, leads to an understanding that all life on Earth is characterized by an integral connectedness from which ecological value flows. If this connectedness is understood to exist in a sacramental universe grounded in the creativity of an incarnational God, the ecological value attributed to the evolutionary epic as the source of all nature and culture can potentially be enhanced even further.

Therefore, the responsibility of the Christian priesthood is not only to provide the administration of the formal sacraments of the Church but also to facilitate the awareness that we live in a world filled with the potential recognition of sacramental grace.[233] Brown's theology of sacrament and tradition provides a framework that makes this possible in a way that can significantly contribute to the expansion of ecological value as well as the influence and renewal of Christian tradition in our modern, pluralistic context. Far from this being a detriment to Christian tradition, reaching out to and engaging with the broader cultural and ecological realities beyond the boundaries of the Church can potentially also reorient the increasingly secular aspects of culture to the beauties of Christian tradition. As a result, the broadening of sacramental tradition can be mutually beneficial both for the relevance and strength of the tradition and for the value for and protection of the life that emerges from our sacramental universe.[234]

In an essay addressing Brown's work on the materially mediated experience of the divine, Mark Wynn states the following: "If human experience can be reclaimed in this sense, and if it is the Christian God who comes to be revealed in the 'reenchanted' world, then material forms will no longer be encountered as brute or threatening presences but will instead speak to us in the accents of love."[235] In Brown's words, "Grace operates everywhere, if only our minds and hearts can be generous enough to allow our eyes to perceive it."[236] To end this chapter where we started with the words of Darwin, such a sacramental view of divine grace revealed through life on Earth is indeed "most beautiful and most wonderful."

Conclusion

From Thomas Berry's perspective, the "universe itself is the primary sacred community. All religious expression by humans should be considered participation in the religious aspect of the universe itself. We are," according to Berry, "moving from the theology and anthropology of religions to the cosmology of religions."[237] Essentially, this is what I have attempted to accomplish here by arguing for a sacramental understanding that extends the theological conversation beyond the human practice of institutional sacraments to include recognition of the divine grace present in all of life. It is, to state the primary point of my argument as succinctly as possible, about valuing life and the evolutionary and ecological processes that are necessary for the perpetuation of a sustainable and robust Earthly biodiversity.

In E. O. Wilson's recent book entitled *Half Earth: Our Planet's Fight for Life*, he argues that we need to set aside half of the world's surface as a refuge for nature in order to protect Earth's threatened biodiversity.[238] Following its publication, he wrote the following in a New York Times' article stressing the importance of focusing on life itself if we are to save life and realize what he refers to as the dream of biological diversity:

> But today the dream is at risk. Civilization is at last turning green, albeit only pale green. Our attention remains focused on the physical environment—on pollution, the shortage of freshwater, the shrinkage of arable land and, of course, the great, wrathful demon that threatens all our lives, human-forced climate change. But Earth's living environment, including all its species and all the ecosystems they compose, has continued to receive relatively little attention. This is a huge mistake. If we save the living environment of Earth, we

will also save the physical, nonliving environment, because each depends on the other. But if we work to save only the physical environment, as we seem bent on doing, we will lose them both.[239]

Is the valuation of life not what we experience as sacramental Christians when we celebrate the Eucharist? As I have attempted to demonstrate in the foregoing chapters, the Eucharistic sacrament should be extended beyond the walls of the church in which it is being celebrated and beyond the historical tradition from which it emerged so that the primary liturgical ritual of the church can effectively reflect not only ecclesiastical but also ecological and cosmic significance. In the Eucharist, Christianity reflects upon the theological understandings of Creation, Redemption, and Resurrection as they have been passed down to us in Christian tradition but also potentially points toward a broader reflection of the perpetuation of the creative emergence of life from death that is characteristic of the evolutionary epic. In our participation in the sacrament, we can recognize the harsher realities of life yet celebrate the fact that we have life at all both in relation to our daily, individual lives and to the interconnected web of life in the world in which we exist.

One of my earliest memories of hearing the theological significance of the Easter story was my mother relating the resurrection of Jesus to the blooming of the dogwoods, with their white blossoms marked at petals' edge with just a touch of crimson, that lined part of the back yard of my childhood home. Would it be so difficult to expand this sacramental image to include a recognition of grace and value in all of the life-giving ecology of our planet? From my perspective, it seems that the Christian remembrance of the life and spirit of Jesus and the Church overcoming the death and defeat of the crucifixion seamlessly connects with an awareness and recognition of evolutionary life constantly emerging from death in new and creative ecological forms of living complexity. Furthermore, how can we speak of celebrating and giving thanks for life in the Eucharist if we do nothing to attend to the human caused destruction of life in the biosphere and, with it, the loss of millions of years of genetic heritage of the species all around us? To fail to answer such a question would mean that our sacramental practice is carried out with an outward display of hypocrisy.

What is needed is a sacramental value for ecology and an ecologically oriented sacramental practice. That, I would argue is closer to the realization of God's kingdom than any yet imagined. By bringing sacramental life into the wider world, we tie care and reverence for nature into what has historically been the primary Christian ritual of thanksgiving for life in all of its uncertainty, joy, sorrow, and glory. The mysterious incarnation of Jesus is where we as Christians enter into our spiritual journey along life's winding way, but if we stop there with the understanding of divine presence in the life of Jesus, we will fail to realize the full potential of God's emerging kingdom. A failure to grasp such a broadened vision of divine grace in the world means that we leave ourselves and our tradition susceptible to the criticism that traditional religions have had their day and will not be the most effective means of offering religious expressions to address contemporary environmental concern.

Arguing for the softening of rigid disciplinary boundaries at the university level, Berry claims that "educational institutions need to understand that ecology is not a course nor a program. Rather, it is the foundation of all courses, all programs, and all professions ... Cosmology, or the universe story, is the implicit basis of every particular course or program."[240] While this would be true for all aspects of Christian formation, it is particularly applicable to seminary education. Classes in the evolutionary and ecological development of life on Earth should not be offered as elective courses but should be an integral part of any seminary curriculum that hopes to effectively prepare students for their vocational roles of guiding their fellow Christians toward religiously fulfilling lives in a way that is completely relevant to our contemporary context. Consequently, the understanding of the Eucharistic that is conveyed in seminary education must be grounded not only in biblical and church history but also in Ecology and the cosmic context from which ecological life emerges. If the Eucharist is about thanksgiving for life, wouldn't it make sense to ground this celebration in the best possible understanding of life that comes to us through the best available scientific evidence? In relation to theological education, perhaps the most unfortunate consequence of failing to take such a perspective seriously is the failure to realize the potential of Christian tradition as a vibrant and creative living tradition.

Such a view does not make it necessary for clergy to become professional scientists, but they should be naturalists in the traditional sense of that term as lovers of nature and the life that flows from it, as students and observers of the natural world either directly or, at the very least, students of those who are. Scientists now tell us that the space that we see between the stars in the night sky is far from being an infinite expanse of empty space but is instead filled completely with billions of galaxies whose stars' light does not reach us. Given the immensity of the cosmos, it is probable that there is life elsewhere in our universe. Yet, we are responsible for only our small place in the universe and for giving thanks for, celebrating, protecting, and preserving the abundance of life that has arisen on Earth. It is then the responsibility of the priest administering the sacraments to make a commitment to align our liturgical worship with the grace that has emanated for some 14 billion years in our sacramental universe which has led to life on Earth. The alignment of the sacramental with the natural is, I would argue, an ennobling, albeit for some frightening, view of the sacraments.

As I approach the conclusion of this study, I think it will be helpful to return to a passage from Wilson cited earlier. In describing the loss of his childhood faith in an understanding of supernatural grace, he writes the following:

> The still faithful might say I never truly knew grace, never had it; but they would be wrong. The truth is that I found it and abandoned it. In the years following I drifted away from the church, and my attendance became desultory. My heart continued to believe in the light and the way, but increasingly in the abstract, and I looked for grace in some other setting. By the time I entered college at the age of seventeen, I was absorbed in natural history almost to the exclusion of everything else. I was enchanted with science as a means of explaining the physical world. In essence, I still longed for grace, but rooted solidly on Earth.[241]

The context of this quote is Wilson's story of his baptism as a young boy in which the very physical nature of his baptism through immersion led him to pose the question, "Was the whole world completely physical, after all?" The result of this question, he continues, was that "something small somewhere cracked. I had been holding an exquisite, perfect spherical jewel in my hand, and now, turning it over in a certain light, I discovered a ruinous fracture."[242]

If we can commit to deeply delving into the mystery and miracle of the Eucharist and the emergence of life on Earth, I propose that the intellectual dilemma between sacramental grace and natural value that posed a stumbling block for Wilson can be reconciled. If grace is understood to be natural, it does not need to be relegated to any notion of a natural/supernatural, physical/spiritual dichotomy. When grace is accepted as natural, the physical also becomes spiritual, which should allow us to cultivate awareness that the divine is present, incarnate in nature and that the natural is so wonderful and awe inspiring as to have no need for the supernatural. Therefore, as we gather at the Eucharistic table to give thanks for and celebrate the beautiful mystery of the gift of life, may we join with E. O. Wilson in affirming the creed of biophilia that "to the degree that we come to understand other organisms, we will place a greater value on them, and on ourselves."[243] In so doing, we can have in mind the grace present in the sacramental ecology of Earth emerging from our ever evolving, creative sacramental universe as we recite the concluding words of the postcommunion prayer from the Book of Common Prayer:

> Send us now into the world in peace
> and grant us strength and courage
> to love and serve you
> with gladness and singleness of heart;
> through Christ our Lord. Amen.[244]

Notes

1   Charles Darwin, *From So Simple A Beginning: The Four Great Books of Charles Darwin*, ed. Edward O. Wilson (New York: W. W. Norton & Company, 2006), 760.

2   Edward O. Wilson, *On Human Nature* (Cambridge Massachusetts: Harvard University Press, 1978), 201.

3   Edward O. Wilson, *Biophilia* (Cambridge, Massachusetts: Harvard University Press, 1984), 1-2.

4   Thomas Berry, *The Sacred Universe: Earth, Spirituality, and Religion in the Twenty-First Century* (New York: Columbia University Press, 2009), 135.

5   In this book, I will use Epic of Evolution, the term attributed to E. O. Wilson, to describe this narrative. However, it should be noted that this narrative has also been assigned different titles including but not limited to the Universe Story, the Journey of the Universe, and Big History.

6   An early version of this chapter was presented as a talk co-sponsored by the University of Georgia Environmental Ethics Certificate Program and Emmanuel Episcopal Church's Steeple and Sidewalk Lecture Series in Athens, GA on October 9, 2012.

7   Frank B. Golley, *A Primer for Environmental Literacy* (New Haven: Yale University Press, 1998), xiii.

8   Edward O. Wilson, *On Human Nature* (Cambridge Massachusetts: Harvard University Press, 1978), 201.

9   Edward O. Wilson, *Consilience: The Unity of Knowledge* (New York: Vintage Books, 1998), 265.

10 Wilson, *Consilience*, 264.

11 See Edward O. Wilson, *The Social Conquest of Earth* (New York: W. W. Norton & Company, 2012), 266.

12 Wilson, *Consilience*, 6.

13 The causes of this human induced biological destruction

are summarized by Wilson with the acronym HIPPO representing the following ecologically destructive forces: *Habitat Destruction, Invasive Species, Pollution, Population, Overharvesting.* See E. O. Wilson, *The Future of Life* (New York: Vintage Books, 2002), 50.

14 Edward O. Wilson, *The Creation: An Appeal to Save Life on Earth* (New York: W. W. Norton & Company, 2007), 4–5.

15 E. O. Wilson, *The Future of Life* (New York: Vintage Books, 2002), 131. Furthermore, Wilson claims, because humans are inextricably linked to the natural environments from which our species emerged, the protection of biodiversity is not to be understood as separate from human welfare. Instead, "a sense of genetic unity, kinship, and deep history are among the values that bond us to the living environment. They are survival mechanisms for ourselves and our species. To conserve biological diversity is an investment in immortality." See Wilson, *The Future of Life*, 133.

16 Wilson, *The Creation*, 26. For an example of his use of the rhetoric of the sacred, see Steve Paulson, "Religious Belief Itself Is An Adaption," *Salon.com*, Tuesday, Mar. 21, 2006, http://www.salon.com/2006/03/21/wilson_19/. Additionally, Wilson claims that our attraction to and valuation of nature is a product of our evolutionary development, a concept that he names "biophilia." He defines "biophilia" as our evolutionary "innate tendency to focus on life and lifelike processes" and claims that "to the degree that we come to understand other organisms, we will place a greater value on them, and on ourselves." See Wilson, *Biophilia* (Cambridge Massachusetts: Harvard University Press, 1984) 1, 2.

17 Thomas Berry and Brian Swimme, *The Universe Story* (New York: HarperCollins, 1992), 3.

18 Ursula Goodenough, *The Sacred Depths of Nature* (New

York: Oxford University Press, 1998), xviii.

19 Goodenough, 171.

20 For a good example, see Goodenough's article "Ultimacy" available at the following web link: http://thegreatstory. org/Ultimacy.pdf. A brief examination of this issue is provided in Chapter 2.

21 Goodenough, *The Sacred Depths of Nature*, 171–172.

22 Goodenough, *The Sacred Depths of Nature*, 73.

23 Wilson, *The Creation*, 5.

24 Brian Swimme and Mary Evelyn Tucker, *Journey of the Universe* (New Haven, Connecticut: Yale University Press, 2011), 5.

25 Goodenough, *The Sacred Depths of Nature*, 173–174.

26 Thomas Berry, *The Sacred Universe: Earth, Spirituality, and Religion in the Twenty-First Century* (New York: Columbia University Press, 2009), 136.

27 Goodenough, *The Sacred Depths of Nature*, xvi.

28 Edward O. Wilson, "Foreword" in *Everybody's Story: Wising Up to the Epic of Evolution*, by Loyal Rue (Albany, New York: State University of New York Press, 2000), x.

29 Max Weber, "Science as a Vocation," http://www.wisdom. weizmann.ac.il/~oded/X/WeberScienceVocation.pdf, 20. (accessed December 24, 2016).

30 Donald Worster, *Nature's Economy: A History of Ecological Ideas* (New York: Cambridge University Press, 1995), 181.

31 Worster., 180.

32 This line appears in Alfred, Lord Tennyson's poem "In Memoriam A. H. H."

33 Alfred North Whitehead, *The Function of Reason* (Princeton: Princeton University Press, 1929), 5.

34 Edward O. Wilson, "General Introduction" in *From So Simple A Beginning: The Four Great Books of Charles Darwin*, ed. Edward O. Wilson (New York: W. W. Norton & Company, 2006), 13.

35 Bron Taylor, *Dark Green Religion: Nature Spirituality and the Planetary Future* (Berkeley: University of California Press, 2010), 221.

36 Taylor, 221.

37 Loyal Rue, *Everybody's Story: Wising Up to the Epic of Evolution* (Albany, New York: State University of New York Press, 2000), 39.

38 Rue, 137.

39 For more information on the film, see http://www.journeyoftheuniverse.org/.

40 Lynn White, Jr., "The Historical Roots of our Ecologic Crisis," *Science*, Vol. 155, No. 3767 (Mar. 10, 1967): 1203–1207.

41 Ibid., 1205.

42 Ibid., 1207.

43 See White, 1206–1207.

44 The following is a link to Peacocke's full interview with Robert Wright: http://meaningoflife.tv/video.php?speaker =peacocke&topic=complete.

45 Golley, *A Primer for Environmental Literacy* (New Haven, Connecticut: Yale University Press, 1998), 232.

46 Wilson is given credit for coining the term "Epic of Evolution" in his Pulitzer Prize winning *On Human Nature*, first published in 1978 where he wrote that "the evolutionary epic is probably the best myth we will ever have." Edward O. Wilson, *On Human Nature* (Cambridge Massachusetts: Harvard University Press, 1978), 201.

47 Edward O. Wilson, *Biophilia* (Cambridge, Massachusetts: Harvard University Press, 1984), 1–2.

48 William Temple referred to a "sacramental universe" in his Gifford Lectures. See William Temple, *Nature, Man, and God* (London: MacMillan and Company, Limited: 1951), Lecture 19.

49 Edward. O. Wilson, "Ethics and Religion" in *Consilience:*

The Unity of Knowledge (New York: Vintage Books, 1999), 260–290.

50 Wilson, *Ibid.*, 290.

51 The important distinction between naturalism and supernaturalism is one that I will return to later in this chapter.

52 Wilson, *Consilience*, 289.

53 See Edward O. Wilson, "A New Enlightenment," in *The Social Conquest of Earth* (New York: Liveright Publishing Corporation, 2012), 287–297.

54 Wilson, *The Social Conquest of Earth*, 266.

55 According to Wilson, we have now entered the world's sixth great extinction event, the fifth being the event that led to the extinction of the dinosaurs 65 million years ago, where, if conditions remain the same, half the Earth's known species could either be extinct or seriously threatened by the mid-twenty-first century. With this in mind, Wilson claims that the scientific narrative of evolutionary history is the story that can most effectively achieve the protection of the Earth's biodiversity from the factors that currently threaten it. See E. O. Wilson, *The Creation: An Appeal to Save Life on Earth* (New York: W. W. Norton and Company, 2007), 4–5. The causes of this human induced biological destruction are summarized by Wilson with the acronym HIPPO representing the following ecologically destructive forces: *Habitat Destruction, Invasive Species, Pollution, Population, Overharvesting*. See E. O. Wilson, *The Future of Life* (New York: Vintage Books, 2002), 50.

56 Edward O. Wilson, *On Human Nature* (Cambridge Massachusetts: Harvard University Press, 1978), 201.

57 Wilson, *Consilience*, 289.

58 Wilson, *Consilience*, 6.

59 Edward O. Wilson, *Naturalist* (Washington, D. C.: Island Press, 2006), 43–44.

60 Wilson, *The Creation*, 26, 12.

61 E. O. Wilson, *The Future of Life* (New York: Vintage Books, 2002), 131.

62 Book of Common Prayer, 857.

63 Book of Common Prayer, 861.

64 Book of Common Prayer, 365.

65 See William Temple, *Nature, Man, and God* (London: MacMillan and Company, Limited, 1951), Lecture 19.

66 I am borrowing the language of God as the "source, center, and end" of all that exists from Dr. William L. Power, Professor Emeritus at the University of Georgia, with whom I studied from 2004–2008.

67 Temple, *Nature Man and God*, 478.

68 John Macquarrie, *A Guide to the Sacraments* (New York: Continuum, 1997), 1.

69 Ibid., vii.

70 Offering an ecological interpretation of the Aristotelian notion that "the whole is greater than the sum of its parts," Eugene P. Odum, the so-called father of modern Ecology, famously commented that "the ecosystem is greater than the sum of its parts."

71 Goodenough claims that a planetary ethic is needed to properly address the ecological problems of our time. She writes: "Any global tradition needs to begin with a shared worldview — a culture-independent, globally accepted consensus as to how things are. From my perspective, this part is easy. How things are is, well, *how things are*: our scientific account of Nature, an account that can be called the Epic of Evolution. The Big Bang, the formation of stars and planets, the origin and evolution of life on this planet, the advent of human consciousness and the resultant evolution of cultures — this is the story, the one story, that has the potential to unite us, because it happens to be true." See Ursula Goodenough, *The Sacred Depths of Nature* (New

York: Oxford University Press, 1998), xvi.

72   Goodenough, *The Sacred Depths of Nature*, 11.

73   Goodenough, 170.

74   Ibid., 171–172.

75   Macquarrie, 102.

76   Genesis 1:1–2:3

77   John 1:3–4

78   In his *Worship as Theology: Foretaste of Glory Divine*, Don E. Saliers describes the emergence of the concept of true eschatology not simply as a discourse on the end times but "as a radical openness to the future." See Don E. Saliers, *Worship as Theology: Foretaste of Glory Divine* (Nashville: Abingdon Press, 1994), 51.

79   The best way to gain an appreciation for this is to actually read through the prayers and rites of the Eucharistic liturgy. See *The Book of Common Prayer*, 316–409.

80   While outsiders may scoff at the seeming supernatural character of religious doctrines such as the Creation, Incarnation, Resurrection, they represent, particularly understood in relation to the context of the ancient cultures from which they emerged, profound affirmations of the natural order. The Incarnation, which is the ground and inspiration of our theological and sacramental tradition, is a radical statement that God's grace is revealed in physical form. William Temple was referring to the Incarnation when he wrote: "By the very nature of its central doctrine Christianity is committed to a belief in the ultimate significance of the historical process, and in the reality of matter and its place in the divine scheme." See Temple, *Nature, Man, and God*, 478.

81   In a discussion on Edward Schillibeeckx's reference to Christ as the "primordial sacrament," Macquarrie connects the overall sacramental system of the church with a broader sense of sacramentality as follows: "There is a kind of

hierarchy here ... Christ is the sacrament of God; the church is the sacrament (body) of Christ; the seven sacraments are the sacraments of the church; the natural sacraments scattered around the world are, from a Christian point of view, approximations or pointers which find fulfillment in the sacraments of the gospel." See Macquarrie, 37.

82   Van A. Harvey, *A Handbook of Theological Terms* (New York: Touchstone, 1997), 156.

83   Goodenough, *The Sacred Depths of Nature*, 171.

84   Macquarrie, vii.

85   Owen C. Thomas and Ellen K. Wondra, *Introduction to Theology* (Harrisburg, Pennsylvania: Morehouse Publishing, 2002), 282.

86   Ursula Goodenough, "Ultimacy," *Epic of Evolution Quarterly*, http://thegreatstory.org/Ultimacy.pdf, 24.

87   Incidentally, Wilson actually invokes the language of miracle in describing the beauty and complexity of biodiversity. He writes, "If a miracle is a phenomenon we cannot understand, then all species are something of a miracle. Each and every kind of organism, by virtue of the exacting conditions that produced it, is profoundly unique and shows its diagnostic traits reluctantly." See E. O. Wilson, *The Creation: An Appeal to Save Life on Earth* (New York: W. W. Norton and Company, 2007), 55. Goodenough expresses a similar sentiment with the following: "The celebration of supernatural miracles has been central to traditional religions throughout the millennia. The religious naturalist is provisioned with tales of natural emergence that are, to my mind, far more magical than traditional miracles. Emergence is inherent in everything that is alive, allowing our yearning for supernatural miracles to be subsumed by our joy in the countless miracles that surround us." See Goodenough, *The Sacred Depths of Nature*, 30.

88   Goodenough, *The Sacred Depths of Nature*, 151.

89 See Saliers, 85–105. For example, he writes, "Liturgy is ... a rehearsal of the way we are to become related to one another and to the world. With respect to creation itself, one is brought to awe and wonder and gratitude when, suddenly, the familiar patterns of life are seen afresh." See Saliers, 102.

90 Saliers, 121, 123.

91 Schubert M. Ogden, *On Theology* (San Francisco: Harper and Row Publishers, 1986), 4–5.

92 Wilson uses the theological language of "the Creation," defined by him as "living Nature," to bring science and religion together for the purpose of protecting biodiversity. See Wilson, *The Creation*, 4.

93 Wilson, *The Creation*, 5.

94 I am borrowing the term "sacramental universe" from William Temple who used it in his Gifford Lectures (1932–1934). See William Temple, *Nature, Man, and God* (London: MacMillan and Company, Limited: 1951), Lecture 19.

95 John Macquarrie, *A Guide to the Sacraments* (New York: Continuum, 1997), 135–136.

96 Bruce T. Morrill, *Encountering Christ in the Eucharist: The Paschal Mystery in People, Word, and Sacrament* (New York: Paulist Press, 2012), 69.

97 Paul F. Bradshaw and Maxwell E. Johnson, *The Eucharistic Liturgies: Their Evolution and Interpretation* (Collegeville, Minnesota: Liturgical Press, 2012), 131.

98 Macquarrie, 136.

99 In the previous chapter, I referenced Schubert Ogden's criteria that all Christian theological statements should be simultaneously appropriate to the tradition of which they are a part and credible to the cultural context in which they are applied. See Schubert M. Ogden, *On Theology* (San Francisco: Harper and Row Publishers, 1986), 4–5.

100 Macquarrie describes the potential for and significance

of a variety of meanings for sacrifice as follows: "What is essential is the offering of something to God, but what is offered might be, for instance, the fruits of the earth or even simply the praise and thanksgiving of the worshipper." See Macquarrie, 135. Additionally, referencing the work of Kenneth Stevenson, Bradshaw and Johnson state that "the metaphor of eucharistic sacrifice has several possible referents and can point at one and the same time to the self-offering of the community, to the gifts (bread and cup) that are offered, and to the entire eucharistic action itself, as that which is offered in thanksgiving for God's gift of salvation." See Bradshaw and Johnson 129–130.

101 Morrill, 24. For a more complete discussion of Jesus' reinterpretation of Jewish communion sacrifice, see Morrill, 23–25.

102 Bradshaw and Johnson, 21.

103 Bradshaw and Johnson, 51.

104 Referring to Justin Martyr's theology of the Eucharist from the second century, Bradshaw and Johnson write: "While it is true ... that Christ's suffering is one of the things in remembrance of which Justin believes the eucharistic sacrifice is to be offered, no greater emphasis seems to be placed on that than on thanksgiving for creation or Christ's incarnation." See Bradshaw and Johnson, 46.

105 Macquarrie, 139.

106 I placed quotation marks around "institution" because of the scholarly doubt placed on Jesus' explicit "institution" of the Eucharist. For example, Macquarrie refers to Jesus as the "source" or "founder" of the Eucharistic sacrament. See Macquarrie, 34–37. Additionally, in relation to the gospel narratives accurately demonstrating the origins of the dominant understanding of the Eucharist in the first century, Bradshaw and Johnson state the following: "Even in the Synoptic accounts of the Last Supper there are signs

that the sayings over the bread and cup have been grafted onto an earlier version of the narrative of a final Passover meal of which they formed no part." See Bradshaw and Johnson, 21.

107 Bradshaw and Johnson, 23.

108 Bradshaw and Johnson trace an increasing trend in this interpretation to the fourth century. They cite, in particular, Cyprian in the third century as a major influence whose "language certainly paved the way for a closer association between Christ's sacrifice and the Eucharistic offering that we find among fourth-century theologians." See Bradshaw and Johnson, 57–59, 129–136.

109 Bradshaw and Johnson, 222.

110 Bernard Cooke, *Sacraments and Sacramentality* (Mystic, Connecticut: Twenty-Third Publications, 1983), 108.

111 Ibid., 109.

112 Morrill, 4–5.

113 Macquarrie, 136.

114 Ibid., 136.

115 Concerning the broad understanding of Christ's presence in the Eucharist, Macquarrie writes the following: "The presence of Christ in the eucharist is a multiple presence. Since the eucharist always includes a reading from the Gospel, Christ is present in that word. Since it is Christ himself who presides at the eucharist, he is present also in the human minister, the priest, who rehearses the words and actions which Christ used at the Last Supper. Christ is present too in the eucharistic community, who are made one body with him, so that they dwell in him and he in them. And, of course, Christ is present in the bread and wine, over which have been said his words, 'This is my body', 'This is my blood'." See Macquarrie, 126–127.

116 For a more extensive assessment of the debates related to the doctrine of the transubstantiation from the ninth–

thirteenth centuries, see Bradshaw and Johnson, 222–227.

117 For a comment on some of these alternative theological perspectives to transubstantiation including "transignification" and "transfinalization," see Bradshaw and Johnson, 341.

118 David Brown, *God and Grace of Body: Sacrament in Ordinary* (New York: Oxford University Press, 2007), 410.

119 Concerning the continued widespread view of a literalist interpretation of the Eucharistic sacrifice of Christ, Macquarrie writes the following: "In spite of St. Thomas' attempt to construct a reasonable account of transubstantiation, one which should have put an end to the crudely materialistic interpretations that were going around, superstitious ideas continued to gain ground." See Macquarrie, 129.

120 Brown, *God and Grace of Body*, 390.

121 Macquarrie, 131.

122 The last chapter of this book is devoted to an examination of the potential for David Brown's sacramental theology to relate Christian sacramental worship to the ecological value that emerges from an understanding of the connectedness inherent in the Epic of Evolution. In brief, he argues for a broadened notion of sacramentality in which God is understood to be sacramentally present in all aspects of human culture and the entire natural world. For a description of the framework of his sacramental theology, see, in particular, Chapter 1 in Brown, *God and Enchantment of Place: Reclaiming Human Experience* (New York: Oxford University Press, 2004).

123 Brown, *God and Grace of Body*, 409.

124 Ibid., 419.

125 The use of the term "imaginative" is a reference to Brown's *Tradition and Imagination: Revelation and Change* in which Brown uses "imagination" as an interpretive term to

argue that we should not separate revelation and tradition in theological discourse as if biblical revelation holds a monopoly on definitive divine revelation. Furthermore, tradition is understood to be an ever emergent process focused on interpreting the ongoing revelation of God in the world. See Brown, *Tradition and Imagination: Revelation and Change* (New York: Oxford University Press, 1999).

126 Brown, *God and Grace of Body*, 408.

127 Morrill, 1.

128 Bron Taylor, *Dark Green Religion: Nature Spirituality and the Planetary Future* (Berkeley: University of California Press, 2010), 220.

129 As referenced at the beginning of this chapter, E. O. Wilson is given credit with coining the term "Epic of Evolution," and it is worth noting that he implies a sense of mystery in the scientific understanding of life when he writes that the evolutionary epic "can be adjusted until it comes as close to truth as the human mind is constructed to judge the truth." See Edward O. Wilson, *On Human Nature* (Cambridge, Massachusetts: Harvard University Press, 1978), 201.

130 Edward Schillebeeckx, *Christ the Sacrament of the Encounter with God* (New York: Sheed and Ward, 1963), 6, 15.

131 Ibid., 43–44.

132 Ibid., 44.

133 Ibid., 215.

134 Schillebeeckx., 215.

135 In discussing the extension of Eucharistic grace into a wider sacramental universe, we must not forget the understanding of the cosmic dimension of the Eucharist itself. While it points outward toward a broader sense of sacramentality, it also represents, in microcosm, the macrocosm of all of God's continuing creation. Take, for instance, the following statement from Alexander Schmemann: "In the eucharist, the *commemoration* is the gathering together of the entire

experience of salvation, the entire fullness of that *reality* that is given us in the Church and that constitutes our life. It is the reality of the world as God's creation, the reality of the world as saved by Christ, the reality of the new heaven and the new earth, to which we ascend in the sacrament of ascension to the kingdom of God." See Schmemann, *The Eucharist: Sacrament of the Kingdom* (Crestwood, New York: St. Vladimir's Seminary Press, 1987), 221.

136 Pierre Teilhard de Chardin, *Hymn of the Universe* (New York: Harper and Row, Publishers, 1965), 47.

137 Ibid., 48.

138 Teilhard de Chardin, 50.

139 Catherine Vincie, *Worship and the New Cosmology: Liturgical and Theological Challenges* (Collegeville, Minnesota: Liturgical Press, 2014), 91.

140 Sallie McFague, "An Ecological Christology: Does Christianity Have It?" in *Christianity and Ecology: Seeking the Well-Being of Earth and Humans*, ed. Dieter T. Hessel and Rosemary Radford Ruether (Cambridge, Massachusetts: Harvard University Press, 2000), 34.

141 In the previous chapter, I wrote the following: "For those of us who are theists, I do not think that it is difficult to accept that the grace of God is present to all living things whether we realize it or not and also that this grace does not depend on human recognition for it to be efficacious."

142 Lizette Larson-Miller, *Sacramentality Renewed: Contemporary Conversations in Sacramental Theology* (Collegeville, Minnesota: Liturgical Press, 2016), 102.

143 Brown expresses this as follows: "So for God to impact on every aspect of us immanence must also be claimed: God involved in matter. Christians believe that this happened at the deepest and most profound level in the incarnation, but if there is to be a continuing effect this cannot have happened just once, but must relate to all material

existence." See Brown, *God and Enchantment of Place*, 81–82.

144 Teilhard de Chardin, 49.

145 See Matthew 22:35–40, Mark 12:28–31, Luke 10:25–28.

146 Bradshaw and Johnson, 8, 9.

147 In his *A Sand County Almanac*, Aldo Leopold famously wrote that a "thing is right when it tends to preserve the integrity, stability, and beauty of the biotic community. It is wrong when it tends otherwise." See Aldo Leopold, *A Sand County Almanac and Sketches Here and There* (New York: Oxford University Press, 1968), 224–225.

148 Morrill, 9–11.

149 Ibid., 10.

150 Elizabeth Theokritoff, "Creation and the Priesthood in Modern Orthodox Thinking" *Ecotheology* 10.3 (2005): 344.

151 Mission and Public Affairs Council of the Church of England, *Sharing God's Planet: A Christian Vision for a Sustainable Future* (London: Church House Publishing, 2005), 24.

152 Mission and Public Affairs Council of the Church of England, 24.

153 Ibid., 24.

154 John Habgood, "A Sacramental Approach to Environmental Issues" in *Liberating Life: Contemporary Approaches to Ecological Theology*, ed. Charles Birch, William Eakin, and Jay B. McDaniel, 53 (Maryknoll, New York: Orbis Books, 1991).

155 Theokritoff, "Creation and Priesthood in Modern Orthodox Thinking," 360.

156 John Zizioulas, "Priest of Creation" in *Environmental Stewardship: Critical Perspectives—Past and Present*, ed. R. J. Berry, 286 (New York: T & T International, 2006).

157 Paulos Gregorios, *The Human Presence: An Orthodox View of Nature* (Geneva: World Council of Churches, 1978), 8.

158 Philip Sherrard, *The Rape of Man and Nature: An Enquiry*

into the Origins and Consequences of Modern Science (Ipswich, Suffolk: Golgonooza Press, 1987), 40.

159 Sherrard, 15.

160 Michael S. Northcott, *The Environment and Christian Ethics* (Cambridge: Cambridge University Press, 2001), 132.

161 Ibid., 133.

162 Theokritoff, "Creation and Priesthood in Modern Orthodox Thinking," 352.

163 Ibid., 360.

164 Theokritoff, "Creation and Priesthood in Modern Orthodox Thinking," 356.

165 Theokritoff, "Creation and Priesthood in Modern Orthodox Thinking," 352.

166 Ian G. Barbour, *Religion and Science: Historical and Contemporary Issues* (New York: HarperCollins Publishers, 1997), 103.

167 Arthur Peacocke, *All That Is: A Naturalistic Faith for the Twenty-First Century* (Minneapolis: Fortress Press, 2007), 52.

168 Peacocke, 43.

169 Ibid., 52.

170 Ibid., 53.

171 Habgood, 51.

172 Theokritoff, "Creation and Priesthood in Modern Orthodox Thinking," 357.

173 Ibid., 356.

174 Theokritoff, "Creation and Priesthood in Modern Orthodox Thinking," 358.

175 Habgood, 48.

176 Habgood, 48.

177 Elizabeth Theokritoff, *Living in God's Creation: Orthodox Perspectives on Ecology* (Crestwood, New York: St. Vladimir's Seminary Press, 2009), 218.

178 Laura Yordy, *Green Witness: Ecology, Ethics, and the Kingdom*

of God (Eugene, Oregon: Cascade Books, 2008), 150.

179 Habgood, 53.
180 Theokritoff, *Living in God's Creation*, 215.
181 Northcott, 145.
182 Theokritoff, "Creation and Priesthood in Modern Orthodox Thinking," 354.
183 Theokritoff, *Living in God's Creation*, 218.
184 Habgood, 51.
185 Charles Darwin, *From So Simple A Beginning: The Four Great Books of Charles Darwin*, ed. Edward O. Wilson (New York: W. W. Norton & Company, 2006), 760.
186 Biologist Edward O. Wilson is given credit with coining term "Epic of Evolution" in his *On Human Nature* where he wrote that "the evolutionary epic is probably the best myth we will ever have. It can be adjusted until it comes as close to truth as the human mind is constructed to judge the truth." See Edward O. Wilson, *On Human Nature* (Cambridge, Massachusetts: Harvard University Press, 1978), 201.
187 I will therefore be arguing against Rowan Williams' claim that we should predicate our understanding of the sacraments primarily on human cultural creativity and not on "some general principle of the world as 'naturally' sacramental or epiphanic." See Rowan Williams, *On Christian Theology* (Malden, Massachusetts: Blackwell Publishing, 2000), 201.
188 In Chapter Two, I referenced Schubert Ogden's criteria that all Christian theological statements must be both appropriate to the tradition of which they are inextricably a part and credible to our contemporary experience. See Schubert Ogden, *On Theology* (San Francisco: Harper and Row Publishers, 1986), 4–5.
189 David Brown, *God and Enchantment of Place: Reclaiming Human Experience* (New York: Oxford University Press,

2004). Brown defines sacramentality as "the view that material reality can point beyond itself to some kind of transcendent reality." See David Brown, "Sacramentality" in *The Oxford Handbook of Theology and Modern European Thought*, ed. Nicholas Adams, George Pattison, and Graham Ward (2013): 1 (PDF version), accessed July 19, 2016, DOI: 10.1093/oxfordhb/9780199601998.013.0030.

190 Brown, *God and Enchantment of Place*, 27.

191 Ibid., 26.

192 Ibid., 22. Additionally, the term "sacramental universe" is borrowed from William Temple who used it in his Gifford Lectures. See William Temple, *Nature, Man, and God* (London: MacMillan and Company, Limited: 1951), Lecture 19.

193 Brown, *God and Enchantment of Place*, 9.

194 Ibid., 2.

195 Brown does not always use such explicitly ecological language; however, the implications of his sacramental theology thoroughly support the use of such terminology.

196 Brown, *God and Enchantment of Place*, 5, 16–18.

197 In a talk presented for the Environmental Ethics Certificate Program at the University of Georgia in October, 2012, I argued that the ecological, geographical, and genetic connectedness that emerges from the Epic of Evolution can lead to a renewed sense of value for and therefore re-enchantment of the natural environment. A revised portion of this talk is included as a significant portion of the first chapter of this book.

198 Brown, *God and Enchantment of Place*, 413.

199 Brown, *God and Enchantment of Place*, 9.

200 Ibid., 33.

201 Toward the end of this chapter, I will further discuss the integral and essential role that the Eucharist plays in the life of Christians in connecting them to God's grace

conveyed through material reality and to the ecological value emerging from the broader sense of sacramentality connected with the Epic of Evolution.

202 Brown, *God and Enchantment of Place*, 410.

203 For example, he writes: "But if all this argues for a conceptualization that precludes automatic narrowing to within Christianity's own borders, it is not easy to produce an acceptable definition for such a range. Some suggest that the attempt should in any case be abandoned." See Brown, *God and Enchantment of Place*, 30.

204 Brown, *God and Enchantment of Place*, 410.

205 In Chapter Two, I wrote the following concerning the relationship of tradition with the Epic of Evolution: "The very meaning of tradition implies that our faith must be applied anew to shape and shape us in the cultures we find ourselves in in our contemporary context."

206 David Brown, *Tradition and Imagination: Revelation and Change* (New York: Oxford University Press, 1999), 1.

207 Brown, *Tradition and Imagination*, 8.

208 Ibid., 1–2.

209 Brown claims that "the Enlightenment continues to require of us an open tradition that is willing to learn from approaches beyond the narrow compass of the Christian community itself." See Brown, *Tradition and Imagination*, 7.

210 Brown, *Tradition and Imagination*, 72.

211 Brown, *Tradition and Imagination*, 106.

212 Ibid., 104.

213 Alfred North Whitehead, *Science and the Modern World* (New York: The Free Press, 1967), 192.

214 Robert MacSwain, "'A generous God': the sacramental vision of David Brown," *International Journal for the Study of the Christian Church*, 15:2 (2015), 140, accessed July 25, 2016, DOI: 10.1080/1474225X.2015.1060401.

215 Ibid., 140.

216 Bron Taylor, *Dark Green Religion: Nature Spirituality and the Planetary Future* (Berkeley: University of California Press, 2010), ix, 221.

217 Taylor, 221.

218 Thomas Berry, *The Sacred Universe: Earth, Spirituality, and Religion in the Twenty-First Century* (New York: Columbia University Press, 2009), 158.

219 Ibid., 98.

220 Ibid., 97.

221 Berry,136.

222 David Brown, *God of Grace and Body: Sacrament in Ordinary* (New York: Oxford University Press, 2007), 4. In Section III, Brown provides a more complete discussion of the necessity of accepting the "physicality" of the Eucharistic sacrament.

223 Brown, *God and Enchantment of Place*, 409.

224 Brown, *Tradition and Imagination*, 101.

225 Brown, *God and Enchantment of Place*, 6.

226 Ibid., 8.

227 Brown, *God and Enchantment of Place*, 410.

228 See Brown, *God and Enchantment of Place*, 409. Elsewhere, he writes: "In his generosity he makes himself available to human beings in every possible context, simply in virtue of the fact that he is creator of it all." See Brown, *God of Grace and Body*, 427.

229 Brown, *God and Enchantment of Place*, 81–82.

230 In his assessment of Trevor Hart's critique that the sacramental is developed in Brown's thought at the expense of a more thorough explication of the incarnation, Robert MacSwain suggests that it may be more appropriate to view "sacrament" and "incarnation" in Brown's sacramental theology as "mutually interpreting terms: incarnation is sacramental and sacrament is incarnational." See MacSwain, 147–148.

231 Brown, *God and Enchantment of Place*, 30.

232 Ibid., 23.

233 In the previous chapter, I wrote that one of the roles of the priestly office is the "cultivation ... of the awareness of the sacramental nature of the creation itself as it is revealed to us in our daily lives." Furthermore, in this capacity, "the role of the priest is to point toward and orient the community of the Church to the presence of divine grace in the elements of the bread and wine, which also serve as a representative example of the divine grace present within all of creation."

234 Addressing the former, Brown provides the following comment: "The more separate and isolated the Bible and liturgy are kept, the more likely it is that the decline of religion will be accelerated, and its contribution marginalized to only a small element in human life." See Brown, *God of Grace and Body*, 427.

235 Mark Wynn, "Re-enchanting the World: The Possibility of Materially Mediated Religious Experience" in *Theology, Aesthetics, and Culture: Responses to the Work of David Brown*, ed. Robert MacSwain and Taylor Worley (2013): 16-17 (PDF version), accessed July 19, 2016, DOI: 10.1093/acprof:oso/9780199646821.001.0001.

236 Brown, *God and Grace of Body*, 422.

237 Thomas Berry, *The Sacred Universe: Earth, Spirituality, and Religion in the Twenty-First Century* (New York: Columbia University Press, 2009), 117.

238 Edward O. Wilson, *Half-Earth: Our Planet's Fight for Life* (New York: Liveright Publishing Corporation, 2016.

239 Edward O. Wilson, "The Global Solution to Extinction," *The New York Times*, March 12, 2016, http://www.nytimes.com/2016/03/13/opinion/sunday/the-global-solution-to-extinction.html?_r=1.

240 Berry, *The Sacred Universe*, 137–138.

241 Edward O. Wilson, *Naturalist* (Washington, D. C.: Island Press, 2006), 43–44.

242 Ibid., 43.

243 Edward O. Wilson, *Biophilia* (Cambridge, Massachusetts: Harvard University Press, 1978), 2.

244 *Book of Common Prayer*, 365.

Bibliography

Barbour, Ian G. *Religion and Science: Historical and Contemporary Issues*. New York: HarperCollins Publishers, 1997.

Berry, Thomas. *The Sacred Universe: Earth, Spirituality, and Religion in the Twenty-First Century*. New York: Columbia University Press, 2009.

Berry, Thomas and Brian Swimme. *The Universe Story*. New York: HarperCollins, 1992.

Book of Common Prayer. New York: Church Publishing Incorporated, 2007.

Bradshaw, Paul F. and Maxwell Johnson. *The Eucharistic Liturgies: Their Evolution and Interpretation*. Collegeville, Minnesota: Liturgical Press, 2012.

Brown, David. *God and Enchantment of Place: Reclaiming Human Experience*. New York: Oxford University Press, 2004.

—. *God and Grace of Body: Sacrament in Ordinary*. New York: Oxford University Press, 2007.

—. "Sacramentality" in *The Oxford Handbook of Theology and Modern European Thought*. Edited by Nicholas Adams, George Pattison, and Graham Ward (2013): 1–20 (PDF version). Accessed July 19, 2016. DOI: 10.1093/oxfordhb/9780199601998.013.0030.

—. *Tradition and Imagination: Revelation and Change*. New York: Oxford University Press, 1999.

The Church of England's Mission and Public Affairs Council. *Sharing God's Planet: A Christian Vision for a Sustainable Future*. London: Church House Publishing, 2005.

Cooke, Bernard. *Sacraments and Sacramentality*. Mystic, Connecticut: Twenty-Third Publications, 1983.

Darwin, Charles. *From So Simple A Beginning: The Four Great Books of Charles Darwin*. New York: W. W. Norton & Company,

2006.

Golley, Frank B. *A Primer for Environmental Literacy*. New Haven: Yale University Press, 1998.

Goodenough, Ursula. *The Sacred Depths of Nature*. New York: Oxford University Press, 1998.

—. "Ultimacy." In *Epic of Evolution Quarterly*, by Ursula Goodenough, 24–25. http://thegreatstory.org/Ultimacy.pdf.

Gregorios, Paulos. *The Human Presence: An Orthodox View of Nature*. Geneva: World Council of Churches, 1978.

Habgood, John. "A Sacramental Approach to Environmental Issues" in *Liberating Life: Contemporary Approaches to Ecological Theology*, edited by Charles Birch, William Eakin, and Jay B. McDaniel, 46–53. Maryknoll, New York: Orbis Books, 1991.

Harvey, Van A. *A Handbook of Theological Terms*. New York: Touchstone, 1997.

Larson-Miller, Lizette. *Sacramentality Renewed: Contemporary Conversations in Sacramental Theology*. Collegeville, Minnesota: Liturgical Press, 2016.

Leopold, Aldo. *A Sand County Almanac and Sketches Here and There*. New York: Oxford University Press, 1968.

Macquarrie, John. *A Guide to the Sacraments*. New York: Continuum, 1997.

MacSwain, Robert. "'A generous God': the sacramental vision of David Brown." *International Journal for the Study of the Christian Church* 15:2 (2015): 139–150. Accessed July 25, 2016. DOI: 10.1080/1474225X.2015.1060401.

McFague, Sallie. "An Ecological Christology: Does Christianity Have it?" In *Christianity and Ecology: Seeking the Well-Being of Earth and Humans*, edited by Dieter T. Hessel and Rosemary Radford Ruether, 29–45. Cambridge, Massachusetts: Harvard University Press, 2000.

MeaningofLife.tv. "Arthur Peacocke," http://meaningoflife.tv/video.php?speaker=peacocke&topic=complete.

Morrill, Bruce T. *Encountering Christ in the Eucharist: The Paschal*

Mystery in People, Word, and Sacrament. New York: Paulist Press, 2012.

Northcott, Michael S. *The Environment and Christian Ethics.* Cambridge: Cambridge University Press, 2001.

Ogden, Schubert M. *On Theology.* San Francisco: Harper and Row Publishers, 1986.

Paulson, Steve. "Religious belief itself is an adaptation," *Salon. com*, March 21, 2006, http://www.salon.com/2006/03/21/wilson_19/.

Peacocke, Arthur. *All That Is: A Naturalistic Faith for the Twenty-First Century.* Minneapolis: Fortress Press, 2007.

Rue, Loyal. *Everybody's Story: Wising Up to the Epic of Evolution.* Albany, New York: State University of New York Press, 2000.

Saliers, Don E. *Worship as Theology: Foretaste of Glory Divine.* Nashville: Abingdon Press, 1994.

Schillebeeckx, Edward. *Christ the Sacrament of the Encounter with God.* New York: Sheed and Ward, 1963.

Schmemann, Alexander. *The Eucharist: Sacrament of the Kingdom.* Crestwood, New York: St. Vladimir's Seminary Press, 1987.

Sherrard, Philip. *The Rape of Man and Nature: An Enquiry into the Origins and Consequences of Modern Science.* Ipswich, Suffolk: Golgonooza Press, 1987.

Swimme, Brian Thomas and Mary Evelyn Tucker. *Journey of the Universe.* New Haven: Yale University Press, 2011.

Swimme, Brian Thomas and Mary Evelyn Tucker. *Journey of the Universe.* Directed by Patsy Northcutt and David Kennard. San Francisco: KQED, 2011.

Taylor, Bron. *Dark Green Religion: Nature Spirituality and the Planetary Future.* Berkeley: University of California Press, 2010.

Teilhard de Chardin, Pierre. *Hymn of the Universe.* New York: Harper and Row, Publishers, 1965.

Temple, William. *Nature, Man, and God.* London: MacMillan and Company, Limited. 1951.

Tennyson, Lord Alfred, "In Memoriam A. H. H." The Literature Network, http://www.online-literature.com/tennyson/718/.

Theokritoff, Elizabeth. "Creation and Priesthood in Modern Orthodox Thinking." *Ecotheology* 10.3 (2005): 344–363.

—. *Living in God's Creation: Orthodox Perspectives on Ecology.* Crestwood, New York: St. Vladimir's Seminary Press, 2009.

Thomas, Owen C. and Ellen K. Wondra. *Introduction to Theology.* Harrisburg, Pennsylvania: Morehouse Publishing, 2002.

Vincie, Catherine. *Worship and the New Cosmology: Liturgical and Theological Challenges.* Collegeville, Minnesota: Liturgical Press, 2014.

Weber, Max. "Science as a Vocation," http://www.wisdom.weizmann.ac.il/~oded/X/WeberScienceVocation.pdf.

White, Jr., Lynn. "The Historical Roots of Our Ecologic Crisis." *Science* Vol. 155, No. 3767 (Mar. 10, 1967): 1203–1207.

Whitehead, Alfred North. *Science and the Modern World: Lowell Lectures 1925.* New York: The Free Press, 1967.

—. *The Function of Reason.* Princeton: Princeton University Press, 1929.

Williams, Rowan. *On Christian Theology.* Malden, Massachusetts: Blackwell Publishing, 2000.

Wilson, Edward O. *Biophilia.* Cambridge, Massachusetts: Harvard University Press, 1984.

—. *Consilience: The Unity of Knowledge.* New York: Vintage Books, 1998.

—. *Half Earth: Our Planet's Fight for Life.* New York: Liveright Publishing Corporation, 2016.

—. *Naturalist.* Washington, D. C.: Island Press, 2006.

—. *On Human Nature.* Cambridge, Massachusetts: Harvard University Press, 1978.

—. "Religious Belief Itself Is An Adaptation." *Salon.com*, March 21, 2006. http://www.salon.com/2006/03/21/wilson_19/.

—. *The Creation: An Appeal to Save Life on Earth.* New York: W. W. Norton & Company, 2007.

—. *The Future of Life*. New York: Vintage Books, 2002.

—. "The Global Solution to Extinction." *The New York Times*, March 12, 2016. http://www.nytimes.com/2016/03/13/opinion/sunday/the-global-solution-to-extinction.html?_r=1.

—. *The Social Conquest of Earth*. New York: W. W. Norton & Company, 2012.

Worster, Donald. *Nature's Economy: A History of Ecological Ideas*. New York: Cambridge University Press, 1995.

Wynn, Mark. "Re-enchanting the World: The Possibility of Materially Mediated Religious Experience" in *Theology, Aesthetics, and Culture: Responses to the Work of David Brown*. Edited by Robert MacSwain and Taylor Worley (2013): 1–18 (PDF version). Accessed July 19, 2016. DOI: 10.1093/acprof:oso/9780199646821.001.0001.

Yordy, Laura Ruth. *Green Witness: Ecology, Ethics, and the Kingdom of God*. Eugene, Oregon: Cascade Books, 2008.

Zizioulas, John. "Priest of Creation" in *Environmental Stewardship: Critical Perspectives—Past and Present,* edited by R. J. Berry, 273–290. New York:T & T Clark International, 2006.

THE NEW OPEN SPACES

Throughout the two thousand years of Christian tradition there have been, and still are, groups and individuals that exist in the margins and upon the edge of faith. But in Christianity's contrapuntal history it has often been these outcasts and pioneers that have forged contemporary orthodoxy out of former radicalism as belief evolves to engage with and encompass the ever-changing social and scientific realities. Real faith lies not in the comfortable certainties of the Orthodox, but somewhere in a half-glimpsed hinterland on the dirt track to Emmaus, where the Death of God meets the Resurrection, where the supernatural Christ meets the historical Jesus, and where the revolution liberates both the oppressed and the oppressors.

Welcome to Christian Alternative... a space at the edge where the light shines through.
If you have enjoyed this book, why not tell other readers by posting a review on your preferred book site.
Recent bestsellers from Christian Alternative are:

Bread Not Stones
The Autobiography of An Eventful Life
Una Kroll
The spiritual autobiography of a truly remarkable woman and a history of the struggle for ordination in the Church of England.
Paperback: 978-1-78279-804-0 ebook: 978-1-78279-805-7

The Quaker Way
A Rediscovery
Rex Ambler
Although fairly well known, Quakerism is not well understood.
The purpose of this book is to explain how Quakerism works as
a spiritual practice.
Paperback: 978-1-78099-657-8 ebook: 978-1-78099-658-5

Blue Sky God
The Evolution of Science and Christianity
Don MacGregor
Quantum consciousness, morphic fields and blue-sky
thinking about God and Jesus the Christ.
Paperback: 978-1-84694-937-1 ebook: 978-1-84694-938-8

Celtic Wheel of the Year
Tess Ward
An original and inspiring selection of prayers combining
Christian and Celtic Pagan traditions, and interweaving their
calendars into a single pattern of prayer for every morning
and night of the year.
Paperback: 978-1-90504-795-6

Christian Atheist
Belonging without Believing
Brian Mountford
Christian Atheists don't believe in God but miss him: especially
the transcendent beauty of his music, language, ethics, and
community.
Paperback: 978-1-84694-439-0 ebook: 978-1-84694-929-6

Compassion Or Apocalypse?
A Comprehensible Guide to the Thoughts of René Girard
James Warren
How René Girard changes the way we think about God and the
Bible, and its relevance for our apocalypse-threatened world.
Paperback: 978-1-78279-073-0 ebook: 978-1-78279-072-3

Diary Of A Gay Priest
The Tightrope Walker
Rev. Dr. Malcolm Johnson
Full of anecdotes and amusing stories, but the Church is still a
dangerous place for a gay priest.
Paperback: 978-1-78279-002-0 ebook: 978-1-78099-999-9

Do You Need God?
Exploring Different Paths to Spirituality Even For Atheists
Rory J.Q. Barnes
An unbiased guide to the building blocks of spiritual belief.
Paperback: 978-1-78279-380-9 ebook: 978-1-78279-379-3

Readers of ebooks can buy or view any of these bestsellers by
clicking on the live link in the title. Most titles are published
in paperback and as an ebook. Paperbacks are available in
traditional bookshops. Both print and ebook formats are
available online.

Find more titles and sign up to our readers' newsletter at
http://www.johnhuntpublishing.com/christianity
Follow us on Facebook at
https://www.facebook.com/ChristianAlternative